# OUT OF THE BOX

# OUT OF THE BOX

Unconventional Fly-Fishing Strategies
and Winning Combinations
to Catch More Fish

## JOHN BARR

STACKPOLE
BOOKS

Essex, Connecticut
Blue Ridge Summit, Pennsylvania

# STACKPOLE BOOKS

An imprint of Globe Pequot, the trade division of
The Rowman & Littlefield Publishing Group, Inc.
4501 Forbes Blvd., Ste. 200
Lanham, MD 20706
www.rowman.com

Distributed by NATIONAL BOOK NETWORK

British Library Cataloguing in Publication Information available

**Library of Congress Cataloging-in-Publication Data**
Names: Barr, John, 1944– author.
Title: Out of the box : unconventional fly-fishing strategies and winning
   combinations to catch more fish / John Barr.
Description: Guilford, Connecticut : Stackpole Books, [2022] | Summary:
   "Fly expert John Barr takes the tactic of fishing multiple flies to
   increase anglers' chances of catching fish to a whole new level.
   Includes chapters on fishing the major hatches, streamer fishing,
   fishing for warmwater species, lake fishing, and insights into how the
   top 10 percent of anglers catch 90 percent of the fish"— Provided by
   publisher.
Identifiers: LCCN 2021058262 (print) | LCCN 2021058263 (ebook) | ISBN
   9780811713023 (hardback) | ISBN 9780811771542 (epub)
Subjects: LCSH: Fly fishing.
Classification: LCC SH456 .B294 2022 (print) | LCC SH456 (ebook) | DDC
   688.7/9124–dc23/eng/20211223
LC record available at https://lccn.loc.gov/2021058262
LC ebook record available at https://lccn.loc.gov/2021058263

♾™ The paper used in this publication meets the minimum requirements
of American National Standard for Information Sciences—Permanence of
Paper for Printed Library Materials, ANSI/NISO Z39.48-1992.

# CONTENTS

# INTRODUCTION

For many years after I started fly fishing, all I ever used was one fly, whether I was fishing dry flies, nymphs, streamers, or bass poppers. I knew that fishing multiple wet flies at one time was a popular method for centuries, but that method of fishing didn't interest me or really seem applicable to my fishing at the time. I am not sure when I transitioned to fishing multiple flies, but over time I started fishing more and more combos that had two or three flies in them, and today I rarely fish with one fly.

Fishing multiple flies has revolutionized the way that I fish. It not only is more enjoyable for me but is also more effective. JAY NICHOLS PHOTO

For whatever reason, a red Copper John is a deadly pattern in streams and lakes. Sometimes you don't want to overanalyze why a fly works, but I frequently choose that color in a nymphing or Hopper-Copper-Dropper rig.
JAY NICHOLS PHOTO

I've told this story before, in my book *Barr Flies* (Stackpole Books, 2007), but it's worth repeating here because it forever changed the way that I fish. In the early 1990s, my good friend Jackson Streit, who owned Mountain Angler in Breckenridge, and I floated the Colorado River (State Bridge area). As we approached one of Jackson's favorite runs, he skillfully rowed the boat to the far side of the river, and we drifted down the bank so we wouldn't spook the fish. We eddied out at the tail of the run and dropped anchor.

The run was a fishy-looking, gentle, 2- to 4-foot-deep riffle about 50 yards long. We started at the tail, planning to work our way to the head. Jackson walked about 40 feet above me, and we began casting. We were both fishing deer hair hoppers with rubber legs. Quickly, Jackson was tight to a fish. As he was landing the bright, 16-inch rainbow, I noticed that the hopper pattern was dangling above the water's surface. I couldn't imagine how he could have hooked the fish if he didn't hook it on the hopper, and I asked him what on earth was going on. He said he was fishing two flies—a hopper-dropper—and that the fish was hooked on a nymph trailed off the bend of the hopper.

After watching Jackson, and getting him to explain how he rigged the flies, I immediately attached 2 feet of tippet to the hook bend of the hopper and tied a weighted Golden Stone nymph to the tippet. I cast the two flies upstream, and the first two or three times my hopper went under I cursed it for not floating well. I was waiting for a fish to take the hopper. Jackson started laughing and said that a fish taking the nymph beneath the hopper was making it sink. I had forgotten that there was a nymph below the hopper. From that moment on, whenever my hopper sank, I set.

In the years that followed I started fishing more and more combos, and developed fly patterns with this technique in mind. For instance, right after fishing with Jackson, I realized that I needed a more buoyant hopper. The fly, which I designed along with Charlie Craven, became the BC Hopper, to which I would eventually tether the Copper John, another fly that I designed to be fished with multiple flies because of its weight and fish-attracting qualities. Eventually, a complete system emerged for fishing multiple flies, and today, whether I am fishing dry flies, nymphs, or streamers for trout or poppers for bass, I almost always fish a combo. In addition to giving me confidence, and just plain being fun to fish, combos offer a number of advantages over fishing a single fly.

The biggest advantage when fishing combos is you give the fish a choice. Feeding habits are not the same for every fish—even in the same fishery. For example, during a hatch some fish may prefer eating from the surface while others may feel more comfortable feeding subsurface. When fishing for rising trout during a midge, mayfly, or caddis hatch, I always use a dry-dropper combo, with the dry fly imitating the adult stage and a sunk dropper imitating the emergent stage of the insect that is hatching. A big advantage to fishing the dry-dropper combo during a hatch is it gives the trout a choice between the emergent stage and the floating adult stage, and you increase your odds of a grab if both stages are presented and you don't have to try to figure out what stage a particular fish is feeding on. When blind-fishing nymphs under an indicator I always fish at least two flies, sometimes three with the nymphs representing the forage in the lake or river I am fishing.

Along these lines, fishing a subsurface fly underneath a dry fly is an excellent technique for pressured fish. Pressured fish are often reluctant to take a floating adult pattern but will readily snatch up a sunken emerger or pupa. Heavily pressured fish have seen countess dry flies and have been hooked on them more than once. These pressured fish can be very difficult to hook on a dry fly but will often take a sunken emerger or pupa without hesitation.

Another advantage of fishing multiple flies is that one of the flies can serve as an attractor for smaller or more imitative patterns. One of my favorite combos is the Hopper-Copper-Dropper (HCD), which is the technique I use most often throughout

A stunning brown that took
the Black Back Emerger.
LANDON MAYER PHOTO

I spend a lot of time fishing lakes for largemouth and smallmouth bass and other species, and the techniques that I have learned fishing for them also help me become a better trout angler. JAKE BURLESON PHOTO

the season when blind-fishing for trout when no fish are rising. The combo gives a fish the option of a dry fly (the hopper) or the Copper John, which is an effective pattern but also an attractor that draws attention to the third option, the often-small dropper. When streamer fishing for trout or bass in open water, I usually have a dropper behind the streamer. Trout may be attracted to the streamer but not take it, but if there have been aquatic insect hatches, a trailer imitating the nymph or emergent

stage of that insect may get snapped up. For example, if there have been midge or damselfly hatches in a lake, trailing a damselfly nymph or a midge pupa behind a streamer can be very effective.

There are some who feel fishing combos is improper and not keeping with the traditions of fly fishing, or they just like the challenge of using one fly. I respect those opinions, and combos are not for everybody, but I really enjoy fishing them and without question it is a very effective technique, especially for pressured fish. They do present some challenges, but with practice the pros far outweigh the cons, in my opinion.

The biggest problem when fishing combos is the flies and tippets getting tangled, although most tangles can be avoided by making smooth, well-timed casts and having the right line, leader, and tippet setup. Making good casts is important when fishing dry-dropper or streamer combos but much more so when casting nymph rigs with multiple flies or the HCD combo. But fishing combos is fun and productive, and with the proper setup, after some time on the water fishing the combos the casting becomes second nature and tangles are not a big problem. When first fishing combos, start casting with a slow, measured stroke, and as your timing gets better you can pick up the pace.

When using multiple flies there are rarely any problems fighting fish, but I have had a fly that isn't in the fish hang up on structure as the fish is running, which usually ends badly. When a fish is netted the flies that are not in the fish can become entangled in the mesh of the net, and caution is needed when removing the fly from the fish so as not to get one of the other flies buried in your flesh when the fish wriggles in the net. A really good reason to pinch down barbs is when you hook yourself, the fly comes out much easier and with less pain than if the fly had a barb.

When bass or trout fishing and I am fishing tight to the shoreline, cattails, or other structure such as a log, I just fish a single streamer. If the money water is tight to the structure, it is easier to land a single fly inches from your target than trying to gauge where to land the dropper.

Finally, regulations in some states and certain rivers and lakes do not allow you to fish with more than one fly, so check the regulations in your state and where you will be fishing.

In my mind the learning curve for fly fishing is infinite, and throughout my journey I have never stopped learning, always keeping an open mind while continuing to evolve and adapting my craft. Through the years I have fished with beginning, intermediate, and expert fly fishers and have learned from all of them. The information in this book is a compilation of what I have learned during that time, and I am honored to be able to share it with you.

In this book I will share the flies and techniques that work for me, but I believe there are many different techniques and fly patterns for a given situation that will achieve the same desired result, and you simply need to find what you feel the most confident in and comfortable with and what works for you. The techniques you decide to use on a given day are often just how you feel like fishing that day, even though they may not catch the most fish.

Most fly fishers, including myself, pursue their craft seriously, but let's not forget to have fun and enjoy the precious time we have on the water. And remember that you are smarter than any fish, and the only thing that they are better at than you is breathing underwater and swimming.

# 1

# RISING FISH

Trout rise when there is food on or just under the surface of the water. When you see fish rising, most often they are feeding on the adult or emergent stage of mayflies (including the dying spinners), caddis, midges, or the adult stage of stoneflies, which hatch on land and do not have an emergent stage. Fish also feed on the surface when land-based insects, collectively referred to as terrestrials, such as grasshoppers inadvertently end up on the water, but the majority of our dry-fly fishing is when aquatic insects are hatching.

An almost surreal setting on a classic dry-fly flat with rising fish. You need to be super stealthy when getting in position before you make a cast. Generally these conditions require a fairly long cast and a perfect presentation. JAY NICHOLS PHOTO

I believe the most effective technique when fishing to rising fish during a mayfly, midge, or caddis hatch is to fish a combo with a highly visible dry fly imitating the adult and a drowned dropper imitating the emergent stage. Most rising trout feed on both stages during a hatch but some fish prefer the adult and others prefer the emergent stage, and fishing a combo will satisfy all of the risers. Also in general most trout feel more comfortable eating food subsurface than on the surface, and you will increase your chances of a take if you offer them a choice.

When fishing during a hatch, I use a 9-foot 3-weight fast-action rod, a matching WF 3-weight line, a 9-foot monofilament 5X leader, and approximately 20 inches of fluorocarbon tippet to the dry fly and then 6 to 9 inches off the bend of the dry fly to the emerger or pupa dropper. I most often use 6X to both flies. It is easy to break off a fish when setting the hook when using 6X if you are too aggressive, but if your set is smooth and gentle it is not a problem. Since you know when your flies are approaching a rising fish you are targeting, you are prepared when a fish takes one of the flies, which makes it easier to gently set the hook.

Depending on conditions and what flies I am fishing, I sometimes use 5X, such as when fishing a caddis hatch in low-light conditions, which reduces the visibility of the tippet. During a caddis hatch, swinging the adult-pupa combo into a riseform is often used, and a stronger tippet reduces break-offs if a big fish takes the pupa.

Fluorocarbon does sink, but 5X and 6X fluorocarbon does not readily penetrate the surface film and will not sink your dry fly. (Regular monofilament should be used when dry-fly fishing using 4X and heavier tippets.) Fluorocarbon has several advantages over regular monofilament, including being less visible in the water. When trout are feeding on top they are focused and wary, and the less visible your tippet is, the better chance you have of a fish taking one of your flies.

Fluorocarbon is also more abrasion resistant, which is a significant advantage when using light tippets. Tippets can get nicked from structure in the water or from ripping your fly out of a tree or bush, or from a fish's teeth while fighting it. Nicks and abrasions may not be a significant problem with heavier tippet, but even a slight nick on light tippet can result in an unexpected break-off when setting the hook or while fighting the fish. If you see a large fish rising, I recommend you do a quick check of your tippet to make sure it is in good shape before casting to the fish. Very large fish can be hooked and landed on 6X if the tippet is in good shape. Also modern 5X and 6X fluorocarbon is generally stronger than regular monofilament of the same diameter and is also stronger than the early fluorocarbon tippet.

**Facing:** A brown on the Dream Stream section of the South Platte in Colorado that had been sipping hatching *Baetis* next to the bank behind me couldn't resist a Vis-A-Dun (VAD)–Barr Emerger combo. I caught this stellar fish on the textbook dry-fly flat behind me. The nice thing about fishing a hatch on a long stretch of flat water is you can spot a rising trout from quite a distance, whereas you have to be fairly close to see fish rising in a riffle. Fish rising in flat water require a very stealthy approach so as not to send out waves to where the fish are rising, which will put them down. Fish are best approached from below so the little waves created even when carefully wading are carried downstream by the current. JAY NICHOLS PHOTO

# CASTING ACCURACY

In real estate, the three most important things are location, location, and location. Of equal importance when dry-fly fishing during a hatch are accurate casting, accurate casting, and accurate casting. When nymph fishing you can lob an indicator or a Euro setup into a run, let the nymphs drift while watching your indicator or sighter, and recast and do well. It takes some practice, but the casting is not difficult and accuracy is not at a premium. Not to demean nymph fishing—I love to nymph fish—but the casting element for nymphing is not difficult. Streamer fishing requires greater casting expertise, but precise accuracy is usually not critical.

When fishing to rising fish, there is endless conversation regarding patterns, tippet, and where and when to hit a hatch, but being able to accurately and properly present the fly to a rising fish trumps everything. I am not diminishing the importance of pattern, tippet, and hatch knowledge, but making the point that accurate casting and presentation are at the top of the list of variables necessary to having consistent success when fishing to rising fish.

You must develop a casting stroke that works for you and then practice that stroke using targets or fish a lot to instill muscle memory so your stroke becomes automatic without thinking during the cast, which can result in inconsistent presentations. If your casting becomes automatic, you will be able to consistently make clean, crisp, and accurate casts. A good rule to follow when fishing to rising fish is to get as close as you think you can without spooking them. Usually the shorter the cast, the better the chance of making a quality presentation with accuracy.

The ability to make accurate casts is extremely important in fly fishing. Though fishing a single fly makes it easier, over time, and with lots of practice, you can cast very accurately with multiple flies. JAKE BURLESON PHOTO

In addition to discussing the techniques I use during a hatch, I think knowing some basic entomology of the four major groups of aquatic insects not only is interesting but can also give insight on how to more effectively fish during a hatch.

## Mayflies

Mayflies are unique in the insect world in that they have two adult stages. The first stage is the newly hatched adult, called a dun, and then the dun undergoes a transformation into the reproductive stage, which is called a spinner. Adult mayflies are unable to eat or drink so their lives are short, only lasting hours or a day or two. Shortly after transforming into the spinner stage mating takes place, followed by egg laying, and then both the males and females die.

Usually the eggs are dropped or tapped onto the water's surface, but some species crawl under the surface and release the eggs into the water or deposit them onto various structure. Most of the eggs eventually end up on the bottom. The eggs undergo a maturation process and hatch into nymphs, which spend their lives on the stream bottom feeding and growing.

The nymphs are covered by a tough outer layer called an exoskeleton, and as the nymph grows the too-small exoskeleton is shed and replaced by a larger one. As the nymph keeps growing this process is repeated a number of times until it is fully

I use a Vis-A-Dun to imitate all adult mayflies, such as the *Baetis* above. The fly floats extremely well and is easy to see from a distance. JAY NICHOLS PHOTO

Nymphs (above) and emergers are often more important than adults. I use various sizes and colors of Copper Johns and Barr Emergers to imitate them. JAKE BURLESON PHOTO

grown. When the nymph reaches maturity the final molt takes place, the nymph stops feeding, and an incredible transformation occurs. Inside the final exoskeleton, the nymph begins to radically transform its body into the adult mayfly. Exactly how this happens is not totally understood by science, but a greatly simplified explanation is the nymph releases enzymes that dissolve most of its tissue except for cells that have always been in the nymph's body but have been dormant, and these cells miraculously start growing into an adult mayfly. It is unknown exactly what triggers the cells to become active, but they start multiplying and continue to do so until the adult is fully formed and is ready to hatch.

While still encased in the nymphal exoskeleton, the adult swims to the surface.

During its ascent it still looks like the nymph but is actually an adult mayfly covered in the final nymphal exoskeleton. On or near the surface as the adult mayfly gets ready to emerge, it wriggles around and this movement causes the exoskeleton, or shuck, to begin to split open. It can take some time for the struggling adult to fully free itself from the shuck, and as the current carries it downstream the adult is often partially in and partially out of the shuck. This stage where the mayfly has not completely shed the shuck is referred to as an emerger by fly fishers.

Once free of the shuck, the adult mayfly ends up on the surface and floats downriver until its wings are dry, and it flies away to start the cycle over again. Both the helpless emergent stage and the adult floating downriver as its wings are drying are easy pickings for trout and account for many of our opportunities to fish to rising fish.

## FISHING A MAYFLY HATCH

Mayfly hatches are the most storied and arguably the most enjoyable hatch to fish. Countless words have been written about mayfly hatches, and their importance and significance to trout and fly fishers is well deserved. Unfortunately the perception by some is that fishing a mayfly hatch is difficult, and they are unnecessarily intimidated by the challenge. Nuances such as tricky currents, wind, and other variables can create problems, but most of the time if you are a proficient caster and make a good presentation, fishing a mayfly hatch is not that difficult.

What I have found to be the most difficult element of fishing a mayfly hatch is being on the water when mayflies are hatching, because there are so many variables that factor into when or if a hatch occurs. Some hatches are dependable, such as Tricos or those on some spring creeks or tailwaters, but in most rivers you make an educated guess based on time of year and the species and hope you get lucky.

Techniques for fishing mayfly hatches often only reference the adults, but during a mayfly hatch most trout feed on both the emergent and adult stages, and both stages are important to both the fish and

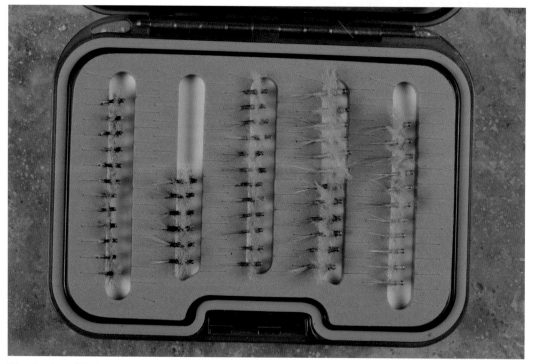

Trico, Baetis, and PMD Vis-A-Duns are staples in my boxes. You can easily match any mayfly with this pattern by changing size and color. JAY NICHOLS PHOTO

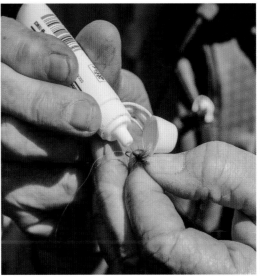

LANDON MAYER PHOTO

JAKE BURLESON PHOTO

There are a number of floatants on the market that ensure your flies stay high and dry. Tiemco's Shimazaki Dry-Shake Spray and Dry Magic are great products to use before your flies get wet. Once flies are wet, I like to use the Dry-Shake powder to revive them.

the fly fisher. Using an adult pattern with an emerger dropper is the most effective technique when fishing a mayfly hatch.

I have been fishing mayfly hatches for many years, and during that time how I fish a hatch has evolved. For years all I used was a single dun pattern, and I would guess that most dry-fly fishers still fish a single dun pattern. This is obviously an effective and enjoyable technique. For me, fly fishing is an evolving process and I am always open to change. After fishing a single dun pattern for years, I started fishing two dun patterns, with the second dun one size smaller and tied on a tippet off the hook bend of the first dun. That approach works, but it gives the trout only the one option of eating a dun, and some trout may prefer eating emergers. Also if the current isn't uniform one of the dry flies can drag, and that causes the other fly to drag. If a dry fly

is dragging unnaturally there is almost no chance a fish will take it.

I then found that a very effective technique was to fish a dun pattern with a sunk emerger tied on a short tippet off the bend of the dry fly. I am convinced that many trout are more willing to take a sunk fly than a floating fly and some trout may just prefer to feed on the emergers. During a hatch I will catch fish on both the dun and emerger patterns. A big advantage to using an emerger dropper comes when fishing to pressured fish that have seen countless dun patterns and have been hooked on them a number of times. Pressured fish that may carefully scrutinize and refuse a floating dun pattern often take the sunk emerger without hesitation. The dry fly serves several purposes. It catches fish, allows you to monitor the drift for accuracy and drag, and acts as an indicator when a fish takes the sunk emerger.

# THE BARR EMERGER

In 1975 while fishing a PMD hatch on
Armstrong Spring Creek outside of Livingston,
Montana, I had a very frustrating experience.
Seemingly every fish in the creek was rising
and eating what looked like little yellow specks,
and ignoring the natural duns as well as my
Light Cahill. Out of desperation I finally put
on my favorite nymph, Polly Rosborough's
Black Drake, and managed to hook a big male
rainbow that had a large, gaping mouth. After
I landed the fish, he opened his mouth wide
and I noticed that the rough part at the base of
his tongue was covered with partially emerged
PMDs. The nymphal shuck still enveloped most
of the insects, with just the pale olive head and
shoulders of the adult PMDs protruding.

The hatch ended, and I went back to my
motel room and set up my vise and tying
materials. I started creating a fly that I hoped
would be a good imitation of the yellow specks
that the trout were eating that day. I based
the design on the partially emerged PMDs
that I had seen on the base of the tongue of
that big-mouthed male rainbow. The fly was
tied on a size 16 dry-fly hook. I started with a
clipped brown hackle tail and a dubbed brown
abdomen to represent the nymphal shuck. I
then tied in some pale olive hackle fibers by
their butts right in front of the brown dubbing.
I dubbed a pale olive thorax, pulled the hackle
fibers over the thorax, and tied the fibers down
right behind the hook eye. I then divided the
hackle fibers and pulled a bunch back on
each side of the thorax and tied them down. I
finished the fly by clipping the hackle fibers so
they extended just past the thorax. The olive

This South Platte beauty chomped a PMD
Barr Emerger. JAY NICHOLS PHOTO

portion of the fly represented the emerging adult PMD. I called the pattern a PMD emerger. At the time I had never heard of the term "emerger," but it seemed like an appropriate name.

The following day I returned to Armstrong. The PMDs started hatching shortly after my arrival and fish started rising and eating the little yellow specks, only this time I knew what was happening. I tied on my new emerger pattern and fished it like a dry fly and hooked almost every fish I cast to, providing the presentation was good. After the hatch was over, I'll never forget how happy I was that the new pattern worked so well, and it continues to be deadly after all these years.

In the years following my discovery, I successfully fished the floating PMD emerger on many rivers. At some point I added a floating *Baetis* emerger pattern, which was as effective as the PMD emerger, but seeing either fly, especially the Baetis version, was difficult if the lighting was not perfect, and I did a lot of guess striking. For years I just fished the emerger as a dry fly during a hatch, but at some point I tied the same pattern on a wet-fly hook, thinking it might be a good pattern when used in a nymph rig, and it turned out to be very effective when used as a nymph.

The next transition came when I started fishing dry-dropper, and tried using the Vis-A-Dun with the emerger as a dropper during a hatch. I tried both the floating and sunk version to see if either was more effective and concluded that they both worked well, but the sunk version was more effective, and I decided that is what I would use. The combo was a real game-changer when fishing a hatch because it gives a trout the option of the dun

or the emerger and allows me to monitor the drift for accuracy and drag, and when a fish takes the emerger, the Vis-A-Dun serves as a strike indicator. From that point on, I always fished a VAD-emerger combo during any hatch.

For whatever reason, trout do not seem to get conditioned to the pattern, and it continues to be effective after all of these years. Before I tied the sunk version and started fishing the dry-dropper combo, I remember two occasions where I caught the same fish twice during the same hatch on a floating PMD. One happened on the Green River and the other on Armstrong Spring Creek. The lighting was good, and I could see the released fish swim back to the same spot where they were hooked, in both cases right off the end of a partially submerged log. The fish started feeding again on naturals and I said to myself, "No way will a fish take the same fly again after just being released." To my surprise, both fish ate the emerger as if they were eating a natural.

In the following years I added a flashback, a bead-head, and a rubber legs version, but the basic pattern has remained unchanged. Lately I have been fishing the Black Back Emerger as my go-to. This is the original Barr Emerger with a strip of black flashback tinsel pulled over the thorax. I don't think it can be called a new pattern, but the black wing case gives the pattern a new look. It is an effective pattern when used as a dropper in a VAD-emerger combo when fishing *Baetis*, *Iswaeon* (formally known as *Pseudocloeon*), *Trico*, or midge hatches. When these insects have been hatching, when the fish have quit rising it is a good choice as a dropper in an HCD setup or as a pattern in a nymph rig.

# Black Back Emerger

- **Hook:** #18-22 Lightning Strike SE5
- **Thread:** Iron gray 8/0 UNI-Thread
- **Tail:** Clipped brown hackle fibers
- **Abdomen:** Brown Super Fine dubbing
- **Thorax:** Adams gray Super Fine dubbing
- **Legs:** Clipped dun hackle fibers
- **Wing case:** Black UTC flashback tinsel

If I am on the water when there is a mayfly hatch, the plan is simple. I look at the mayflies on the water and choose a dun pattern that I think is about the same size and color as the natural and if possible capture a natural and note the body length. Trout get a vague image of the overall size and color of the mayfly, but I feel that the body length of the natural is the most important feature to imitate because as the dun is floating downstream, the trout is looking up at the underside of the insect and the most prominent anatomical feature that a trout sees is the body imprinted onto the water's surface.

For whatever reason, trout can be very selective when eating duns, and maybe the length of the dun's body is an important trigger when a trout decides to eat or refuse an imitation. The wings are vertical and trout don't get a good image of them, and I think trout pay little if any attention to the tail and legs. Some mayflies have big wings and short bodies and can appear bigger to the angler who is viewing the floating dun from above. If you are not sure of what size dun pattern to use and you can't capture a natural, just make your best guess. It is usually better to go a little too small than too big.

Also keep in mind that with an emerger dropper, the adult pattern doesn't have to be perfect. Trout are not as selective when choosing to eat an emerger as they are with the duns. The size of the natural emergers can vary depending on how much of the dun has escaped the shuck, so just pick an emerger pattern that looks to be an appropriate size. I use around 20 inches of 6X to the dun, tie a piece of tippet around 6 to 9 inches long to the bend of the dun, and tie on the emerger.

When I find rising fish, I pick out a fish and position myself so that I can make a good presentation and a clean, unobstructed backcast. I start off with several dead-drift presentations. Keep in mind that a feeding trout doesn't eat every natural that floats over it, so all you can do is hope you have good timing on one of your casts. If I feel the presentation with a dead drift is good but after several casts I get no response, I will add a few little twitches to the flies just before they get to the fish. The twitches can be imparted by the rod tip or with little strips of the line. These twitches will get the fish's attention and make your flies stand out among the naturals.

Don't confuse twitches with drag. Mayfly duns and emergers are alive and do move, especially so with the emergers as they swim to the surface and struggle to escape their shuck. There have been many times when twitching the flies triggered a take from fish that I couldn't fool with a dead drift.

Detecting when a fish takes the dry fly is easy as long as you can see your fly, and when a fish takes the emerger it is like detecting a take while nymph-fishing with an indicator. When a fish takes the emerger, the dry fly will either quiver or get pulled totally under the surface.

If a fish is rising downstream from where I am standing, there is a third option. I will make a dead-drift presentation then add some twitches, and if that doesn't produce I will swing the flies into the fish. I will make a cast above the fish and swing my flies on a tight line, and before the flies get to the fish, I push the rod towards the flies and put some slack into the line. This allows the emerger to sink, and just before the

The Dark Back Emerger is an excellent pattern when used as a dropper in the VAD-emerger combo when light-colored mayflies such as PMDs or Sulphurs are hatching, as the dropper in an HCD, or as part of a nymph setup when the fish have quit rising. It's also a good pattern when used as a dropper under a Puterbaugh Caddis or as a nymph in an HCD or nymph setup if tan microcaddis have been hatching. JAKE BURLESON PHOTO

flies arrive at the fish I will slowly raise the rod tip, which removes the slack and causes the emerger to rise up, which often generates a take.

At times, the most perfect patterns and various presentations do not work, and I just accept the fact that some fish are impossible to fool. These "impossible fish" are usually in ultra-pressured fisheries where the fish have seen countless flies and have previously been hooked more than once,

making them "fly shy." If you make eye contact with some rising fish in these pressured fisheries you can put them down, or even if they keep feeding you have zero chance of fooling them.

There are many good dun and emerger patterns, and I recommend that you use the patterns that you have the most confidence in. A problem with some dun patterns is they can be difficult to see unless the lighting and other conditions are perfect. I feel strongly

that any dry fly must be easily seen after it lands on the water and throughout the drift so you can see if a fish takes your fly and tell if your cast is accurate or if there is any unnatural drag on your fly. If a trout takes the dry fly you want to be able to see the take, and if it takes the dropper you want to be able to see the dry fly quiver or get pulled under.

My confidence dun pattern for all mayflies is the Vis-A-Dun, which is a pattern I have been using for many years. It can be tied in any size and color to match whatever mayfly you want to imitate. I put Comparadun-style white polypropylene wings on all of my Vis-A-Duns, which makes them very visible, even in the small sizes. Natural mayfly duns have dun-colored wings and a pattern with gray wings looks better and more natural, but over the years of fishing Vis-A-Duns with both gray and white wings, I have found that those with white wings were as effective as those with gray wings, so now all of my Vis-A-Duns have white wings. Patterns with gray wings can be difficult to see and follow during the drift, especially if the light is poor.

I don't feel that wing design or color are important to the fish. They are looking up at a drifting natural or imitation and do not get a very clear look at the wings. I think fish key on the overall size, body length, and color of a fly. I like a fairly sparse, short,

My number-one river box when I am fishing for rising trout or using the Hopper-Copper-Dropper system. The left side contains Vis-A-Duns, Puterbaugh Caddis, hoppers, and Copper Johns. The right side contains Black and Dark Back Emergers, PMD Emergers, Graphic Caddis Pupas, and drowned rusty and Trico spinners. The emergers, pupas, and drowned spinners are multipurpose patterns in that I use them both as the dropper in an HCD rig and as a dropper under the dry fly when fishing a hatch or spinner fall. JAKE BURLESON PHOTO

My confidence dun pattern for all mayflies is the Vis-A-Dun, which is a pattern I have been using for many years. It can be tied in any size and color to match whatever mayfly you want to imitate. JAY NICHOLS PHOTO

fanned-out-style tail tied with stiff rooster hackle because it helps float and properly position the fly on the water.

## Caddis

Caddis are widespread and different species can hatch throughout the year, with some species producing mind-boggling numbers of individuals during a hatch. Mayflies are important to trout and fly fishers, but on some rivers caddis are equally or maybe more so. You should always carry adult and pupa caddis patterns wherever you are fishing.

The life cycle of a mayfly has three stages—egg, nymph, and adult—whereas caddis have a fourth stage referred to as a pupa. Unlike mayflies, adult caddis can feed and may live for several weeks.

After hatching, adult caddis mate and the female lays her fertilized eggs in the river. The eggs can be dropped or tapped onto the water's surface, and the females of some species swim under the surface and release their eggs or deposit them onto various structure. Most eggs end up on the bottom, where they mature and hatch into a wormlike nymph called a larva, which starts feeding and growing. The larva's outer layer, or skin, is protective, but it does not have a hard exoskeleton like the mayfly nymph.

The larva continues to eat, grow, and shed its skin like a snake and regrows a new protective skin as it gets bigger until it is fully mature, at which time it stops eating. The larva then finds a safe spot to hide, such as a crevice in a rock or piece of wood, and proceeds to the next stage, which is called pupation. The larva spins a silky sheath around itself and transforms into the pupa stage. While encased in its silky sheath, and in a process much like mayfly nymphs, the pupa proceeds to radically transform its body into an adult caddis.

When the adult is fully developed and ready to hatch, while still encased in its

Free-living caddis larva nymphs. Free-living caddis are an important forage in many rivers, and my favorite pattern to imitate them is my Net Builder Caddis Larva. JAKE BURLESON PHOTO

A caddis adult. My go-to pattern to imitate caddis adults is the Puterbaugh Caddis, which has a high-floating foam wing. JAY NICHOLS PHOTO

pupal skin, it crawls out of its silken sheath and begins its journey towards the surface. At this stage the pupa is actually an adult caddis but still encased in its pupal skin. Pupae can hatch into adults soon after reaching the surface, but most of the time they drift for a while before they are ready to hatch. The adults of some species will escape their pupal covering before reaching the surface and swim up to the surface.

Unlike mayflies, which often struggle to escape their nymphal shuck, once caddis are ready to hatch they shed their pupal shuck rapidly; the adult pops out and floats downriver as the wings dry and then takes off. Maybe this quick exit explains the explosive rises sometimes seen when trout are feeding during a caddis hatch. Since adult caddis leave their pupal covering rapidly, trout don't have a chance to key on the emerging adult, and caddis emerger patterns are not important to the fly fisher.

Pupae are an important food source for trout, and fishing an imitation of a pupa during a caddis hatch is almost mandatory. After adult caddis hatch, they drift downriver on the surface while their wings dry, then fly away, mate, and start the cycle again. While the pupae and adults are drifting, they are helpless and easy targets for trout. Trout feed on both the adults and pupae during a caddis hatch, and fishing a combo of an adult-pupa dropper is by far the most effective technique.

This brown took a Graphic Caddis Pupa right after twitching the dry-pupa combo as it reached the rising fish. JAY NICHOLS PHOTO

# Graphic Caddis Pupa

- **Hook:** #14-16 Lightning Strike SE5
- **Thread:** Olive 70-denier UTC Ultra Thread
- **Butt:** Silver Holographic Flashabou
- **Under body:** Olive 70-denier UTC Ultra Thread
- **Over body:** Green Stretch Tubing (small)
- **Collar:** Brown Hungarian partridge
- **Head:** Dark scud Sow Scud dubbing

## FISHING A CADDIS HATCH

Some rivers, for example the Arkansas River in Colorado, have what's referred to as the Mother's Day Caddis hatch that produces huge numbers of insects, and every fish in the river is feeding on the pupae and adults. My personal experiences with mega caddis hatches have been the Black Caddis on the Big Horn River in Montana and a tan caddis on the Missouri River, also in Montana. The biggest problem in fishing the mega hatches is not what patterns to tie on, but the immense competition from the hatching insects. Whether fishing a mega hatch or a hatch with a normal number of insects hatching, by far the most effective approach is to fish a combo with an adult pattern and pupa dropper.

I fish a caddis hatch the same way that I fish a mayfly hatch. I observe the rising fish, pick out a fish, and position myself so that I can make a good presentation and have a clean backcast. I look at the naturals on the water and select a pattern that closely matches the size and color of the hatching insect. Because of the anatomy of a caddis,

The second of two boxes that I carry when fishing rivers. It contains streamers if the conditions call for a streamer and nymphs that I use when nymph fishing with an indicator. All the flies are heavily weighted and when used as a dropper under a Copper John may tend to sink the hopper. Included are Net Builder Caddis Larva, Stonefly Nymphs, Tung Teasers, and a good selection of Cranefly Larva. JAKE BURLESON PHOTO

# Puterbaugh Caddis (Tan)

- **Hook:** #14-16 TMC 100
- **Thread:** Tan 70-denier UTC Ultra Thread
- **Body:** Tan Fly Foam (⅛ inch)
- **Wing:** Bleached deer hair
- **Hackle:** Brown

I like to use a Puterbaugh Caddis dry fly with a Graphic Caddis pupa dropper combo when fishing a caddis hatch. I like an olive pupa pattern if the adults are dark and a tan pattern if the adults are light. I use three different techniques when fishing a caddis-pupa combo: I can present the combo with a dead drift; dead drift with a twitch or two as the combo nears the rising fish; or if the fish is below me, swing the combo into the fish. This nice rainbow from the Dream Stream section of the South Platte in Colorado took the dry fly during a dead drift. JAY NICHOLS PHOTO

it is easy to determine what size fly to use to imitate the adult. The wings on a caddis are positioned horizontally, lying on top of and extending past the end of the body, and the trout see the wings and body as one unit. The angler looking down on the insect sees the same-length insect as the trout sees looking up at the insect.

The most important consideration when choosing an adult caddis pattern is the overall length and color of the insect. It is important that your pattern matches the length of the adult, but the color only needs to be close. Even though trout feed selectively during a caddis hatch, they don't seem to be as selective as they are when feeding during a mayfly hatch.

There are many good adult caddis patterns but, like a mayfly dun imitation, it must be visible so accuracy and drift can be

monitored. I like the Puterbaugh Caddis. It is buoyant and has a bleached deer or elk hair wing, which is quite visible, and is an effective pattern. I use around 20 inches of tippet to the dry fly and 6 to 9 inches of tippet to the pupa tied off the hook bend of the adult pattern.

There are also many good pupa patterns, but my favorite is the Graphic Caddis Pupa, which I developed years ago and has always been a dependable producer. It is not an exact science, but if the adult caddis is dark I use an olive pupa pattern, and if it is light I use a tan pattern. During a caddis hatch there are both adults and pupae in the drift, and trout feed on both stages.

I use the same three presentations fishing a caddis hatch that I use for a mayfly hatch. If the fish is rising across or above where I am standing, I start with a dead drift, and if that doesn't produce, I add some twitches just before the flies get to the fish. Caddis pupae do move as they swim towards the surface and while they are drifting prior to hatching. If the fish is rising below me, I will dead drift and then twitch if no response, and if it doesn't take one of the patterns, I will swing the adult-pupa combo into the fish. Just like when swinging the adult-emerger into a rising trout, I will make a cast across and downriver above the fish and let the flies come tight, and as they are swinging I push my rod towards the flies, allowing the pupa to sink. Just before the flies reach the fish I get tight to the flies, which causes the pupa to rise up in front of the trout.

Swinging an adult-pupa combo into rising trout during a caddis hatch is a very effective technique. It is so effective that I often position myself above a rising fish and make my first presentation. I like to use 6X fluorocarbon to both the adult and pupa if conditions are demanding, such as flat water and full sun, but I won't hesitate to use 5X to both flies if the fish are large and I am swinging the flies into them.

## Midges

Midges are usually the only aquatic insect that hatch in the winter and during this time provide the only opportunity for fly fishers to fish to rising fish. Although midges provide dry-fly fishing in the winter, they can hatch throughout the year. In the summer I have seen mayflies, caddis, and midges hatching at the same time. In some fisheries such as tailwaters the midge biomass can be incredibly high, and midge larvae, pupae, and adults provide a significant source of forage for trout throughout the year as well as opportunity for the fly fisher.

Midges have the same four-stage life cycle as caddis, consisting of egg, larva, pupa, and adult. After hatching the adult male and female midges mate, and the female drops or taps her fertilized eggs onto the water's surface, where they sink to the bottom. The adults live only a day or two, and both the males and females die after mating and egg laying. The eggs hatch into wormlike nymphs called larvae, just like the caddis. The larvae proceed to feed, grow, and shed

**Facing:** A nice brown that was feeding on caddis and couldn't resist an olive Graphic Caddis Pupa dead drifted under a Puterbaugh Caddis. LANDON MAYER PHOTO

Midges are usually the only aquatic insect that hatch in the winter and during this time provide the only opportunity for fly fishers to fish to rising fish. PAT DORSEY PHOTO

Midge adults (above) can be important food sources for trout, as can the pupae and larvae. JAY NICHOLS PHOTO

and regrow their skin until mature, at which point they stop feeding and find a good hiding place, which is often in the silt on the bottom. Just like caddis, the larvae encase themselves in a silken sheath and transform into the pupal stage.

When ready the pupa miraculously transforms into the adult midge, and while still encased in the protective sheath it swims (wiggles) towards the surface, where it will hatch. Even though the hatching stage is still called a pupa, it is actually an adult encased in the pupal skin. During a midge hatch the pupae usually drift in the current just under or in the surface film for a while before hatching and are quite vulnerable to predation and an easy target for trout.

When ready to hatch, the adult wriggles around inside its pupal covering, which causes the pupal skin to split, and the adult midge crawls out. The exit from the pupal skin is rapid, just like caddis, and a midge emerger pattern is not needed. The adult midge floats downriver on the surface, sometimes skating around while the wings dry. The wings can dry fairly fast, and then the midge flies away, mates, and the cycle starts over.

## FISHING A MIDGE HATCH

For years I fished a midge hatch with a single dry fly, just like I used to when fishing a mayfly or caddis hatch. I used a number of different patterns, most often a Griffith's

This gorgeous rainbow took a midge pupa fished below a Vis-A-Dun. JAKE BURLESON PHOTO

Gnat, but unless the lighting was good, seeing any of the available adult midge patterns, including the Griffith's Gnat, was challenging.

Adult midges fly away soon after hatching and are prone to buzzing around on the surface before they fly off. During a hatch trout feed on both the adults and pupae, but they eat more pupae because they are an easier and more available target than the adult. Nowadays when fishing a midge hatch I use a dry fly and sunk pupa combo, and my success rate has increased significantly over when I just fished a dry fly. I use a black- or olive-bodied Vis-A-Dun as my dry because it floats well and is very visible, even in poor light. Although it is not a classic

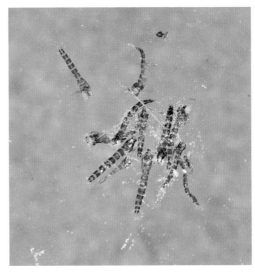

Midge pupal shucks on Spinney Mountain Reservoir, Colorado. JAY NICHOLS PHOTO

midge pattern, it is still taken by midging trout. I use a Black Back Emerger as my pupa imitation. It is not a classic pupa pattern, but I have had no problem with trout taking it as a midge pupa. Trout eat adults and I catch fish on the dry fly, but the majority of the fish I hook during a hatch are on the pupa dropper. I use the same flies when fishing a *Baetis* or Trico mayfly hatch.

I always use 6X fluorocarbon to both flies because midges usually hatch in slower currents and the trout get a good look at the flies, and the 6X fluorocarbon reduces the visibility of the tippet. I use around 20 inches of tippet to the dry fly and 6 to 9 inches tied off the hook bend of the dry fly to the pupa dropper. The dry fly catches fish, serves as an indicator, and allows me to monitor the drift for drag and accuracy. There is no need for an emerger pattern because even though the pupa may drift for a while, the actual hatching into the adult happens rapidly.

I employ the same approach when fishing a midge hatch as I do when fishing a mayfly or caddis hatch. I start with a dead drift followed by some twitches if the dead drift doesn't produce. The natural pupa wriggles around while freeing itself from the sheath that encloses it and the adults can skate around on the surface, so moving the flies does not create unnatural movement. When fishing to rising fish below me, I use the same swinging technique used when fishing caddis or mayfly hatches. The rising pupa pattern right in front of the fish you are targeting can be very effective. During

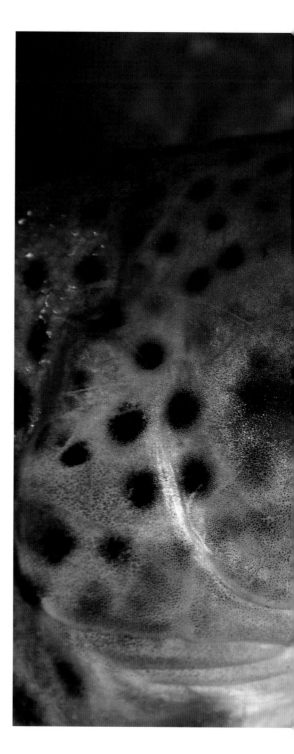

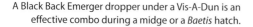

A Black Back Emerger dropper under a Vis-A-Dun is an effective combo during a midge or a *Baetis* hatch.

A nice rainbow feeding tight to the bank was hooked during a *Baetis* hatch on the Poudre River. A Black Back Emerger was taken with confidence by the fish as I twitched the VAD–Black Back Emerger combo just before it reached the fish.

a midge hatch there are often multiple species hatching that can be different sizes, and I don't think that trout key in on any one of the species but rather feed opportunistically on all of them.

## Stoneflies

The fourth group of aquatic insects that is important to fly fishers is stoneflies. The stonefly's life cycle has the same three stages as mayflies—egg, nymph, and adult—however, how they hatch differs significantly from mayflies as well as midges and caddis. Stonefly nymphs don't hatch in the river; rather they crawl out of the water onto structure and hatch.

After hatching stonefly males and females mate, and the female then flies out over the river and drops or taps her fertilized eggs into the water. The eggs fall to the bottom, where they mature and hatch into nymphs. The nymphs are just like mayfly nymphs, with a hard exoskeleton. The nymphs soon start feeding and growing. As they grow they keep growing new exoskeletons to accommodate their increasing size until they are fully mature, at which point they stop feeding and find a good place to hide, which is often under a stone.

The same miraculous transformation then begins within the exoskeleton that occurs with mayflies. Most of the nymph's cells begin to dissolve except for some dormant cells that were always in the nymph, and these cells begin to multiply and grow into a fully formed adult while still encased in the exoskeleton.

Up to this point mayflies and stoneflies have followed the same developmental path, but how stoneflies hatch is radically different from mayflies. Mayfly nymphs swim to the surface and hatch in the river, whereas when a stonefly nymph (actually an adult stonefly still in its nymphal exoskeleton) is ready to hatch, it crawls out of the water onto exposed structure in the river such as a log or onto land and grasps some structure such as a rock or stick, where it will hatch. Usually stonefly nymphs exit the river at night to avoid predation from birds. The adult wriggles around until the

The giant Salmonfly (above) is one of the West's greatest attractions, but Golden Stones and Yellow Sallies are also extremely important. JAY NICHOLS PHOTO

exoskeleton splits, and it crawls out and grasps the structure where it hatched while its wings dry. It then flies away to find a mate, leaving behind its distinct nymphal shuck on streamside rocks and sticks.

## FISHING STONEFLIES

Mayflies, caddis, and midges hatch in the river, and rising trout feed on the emergent or adult form of these insects while they are hatching. Stoneflies hatch on land, thus there are no stonefly emerger patterns, and when fishing adult stonefly patterns you are not fishing during an actual hatch. Except for the occasional rise, most often you are blind-fishing for trout that are on the lookout for adult stoneflies that inadvertently end up in the water.

Stoneflies mate in the streamside bushes and trees, and after mating the female returns to the river and lays her eggs. She flies low over the surface, dropping or tapping her eggs onto the water. Stoneflies are weak, clumsy fliers and many end up in the water and get trapped in the surface film, making them an easy target for trout. Males can also inadvertently end up in the water after falling from streamside bushes, getting blown into the water by wind gusts. When you see stoneflies flying around or over a river, trout will be looking for them in the water, and success can be

No trout can pass up a big, juicy Golden Stonefly nymph, and when the nymphs come out from their hiding places just before migrating to shore to hatch, they become quite available to trout. At this time a pattern imitating them can be a really good choice.

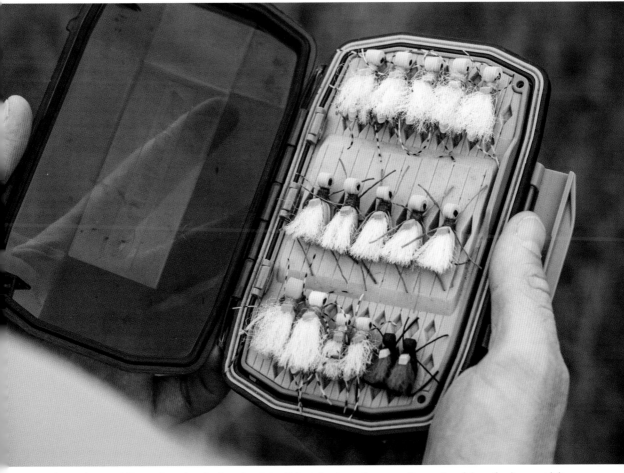

This might sound like sacrilege, but for the sake of simplicity, I simply use hopper patterns when fish are feeding on adult stoneflies. JAKE BURLESON PHOTO

had by blind-fishing or casting to the occasional rise.

Even though large stoneflies get anglers excited, the reality is trout have been eating their normal diet largely consisting of mayflies, caddis, and midges all year and they continue to do so even if stones have been hatching. The occasional large stonefly adult in the water will get eaten and if for some reason a large number of stoneflies end up in the river trout may key on them, but this doesn't happen very often and most of the trout's diet during a stonefly hatch will still consist of their normal forage.

It is fun to fish and anticipate a monster trout eating your large dry fly, but when stoneflies have been hatching I still fish the Hopper-Copper-Dropper, with the dropper imitating the emergent stage of the aquatic insects that have been hatching, and

throughout the day most of the fish will be hooked on the Copper John or the dropper.

If large Golden Stones have been hatching, I like to use Paramore's Thunder Thighs or the BC Hopper, both with a yellow body. If Salmonflies have been hatching, I color the yellow foam body orange with a felt-tipped marker. Trout do not scrutinize floating stoneflies very carefully, and the hopper body gives a good silhouette of an adult stonefly. Keep in mind that during the time the large stoneflies are hatching, it is also prime time for hoppers, and the hopper pattern covers both insects.

Every year I fish the Yampa River near Steamboat Springs, Colorado, in early September. If there are no hatches with rising fish, I fish the HCD setup with a yellow-bodied hopper, a Copper John, and a dropper imitating the emergent stage of the aquatic insects that have been hatching. Large Golden Stones hatch every night and are seen flying around during the day, and no doubt some end up in the river and are eaten by trout. I catch fish on the hopper and whether they take it for a hopper or a stone is impossible to say, but I would guess some of the fish take it for a big Golden adult.

The reality is that the majority of fish are caught on the Copper John or the dropper. One year I was fishing an epic Salmonfly hatch on the Colorado River near Parshall, Colorado, and was fishing an adult Salmonfly imitation with a red Copper John and a PMD emerger dropper, and more fish were

The Rubber Leg Copper John doubles as a stonefly nymph pattern. LANDON MAYER PHOTO

A Salmonfly nymph from the South Platte River. These large nymphs can vary from dark brown to black in coloration.
JAY NICHOLS PHOTO

hooked on the Copper John and dropper than on the adult stonefly pattern.

No stonefly has garnered more attention than the spectacular-looking and super-sized Salmonflies, and they have generated many entertaining stories. A unique phenomenon that occurs in a canyon on the Gunnison River in Colorado is big trout can leave a wet mark on the granite wall when they viciously take an adult Salmonfly trapped in the surface film. Drift boat anglers make a cast so their imitation lands above the splash mark, let it drift, and hope a monster eats it.

I have read and heard tales of monster trout wildly crushing Salmonflies during the hatch on many rivers in the West. Personally I have chased the Salmonfly hatch on many of these rivers, including the Yellowstone and the Madison, when there were numerous adult Salmonflies in the air, and I have never had unbelievable fishing with an adult pattern. I know it happens, and have heard and read many theories on how to time the hatch and have incredible dry-fly fishing, but I have yet to experience it. Even though I have not had great success, it is always fun throwing large dry-fly imitations and anticipating the explosion of a monster trout.

The reality is you can have much better and more predictable fishing with stonefly nymph patterns before the nymphs leave the river. Before hatching, the large stonefly nymphs become very active and leave the security of their hiding places and crawl around on the bottom, staging for their exit from the river. Some of the nymphs lose their grip on the bottom, and since they can't swim, they are helplessly carried downstream. During this time they are easy pickings for trout, and no doubt far more stonefly nymphs are eaten during this pre-hatch activity than are stonefly adults. Trout will also pick them off the bottom. I have wondered what would happen if I used a size 10 black Slumpbuster tied on a jig hook so that it rides hook point up, and crawled it along the bottom of one of these famous rivers before the adults started hatching.

The heavyweights in the stonefly family are the Salmonflies and the large Golden Stones and they get most of the publicity, but the Yellow Sallies are probably the most important stonefly for the fly fisher and the trout, even though they lack the charisma of the giant Goldens or Salmonflies. They are a large group of small tan-to-yellow and yellow-to-green stoneflies that are widely distributed and can hatch, sometimes in large numbers, throughout the season. To imitate the Sallies I like a yellow-bodied Kaufman's Stimulator with a white calf tail topper on the wing. Sizes 14 and 16 are the two sizes I carry, which cover most of the Yellow Sallies. The small Stimulators don't support a Copper John very well, so I will just fish an emerger or pupa as a dropper.

Adult stoneflies can almost be thought of as terrestrials such as hoppers. Both hatch on land and their appearance on the water is unpredictable, but if either has been hatching some end up in the water and trout will be on the lookout for the meaty, nutritious meal.

When fishing the HCD technique I use a 9-foot 4-weight fast-action rod, matching WF 4-weight floating line, and a 7½-foot 2X leader. I tie the hopper to the 2X and use 3 to 4 feet of 4X fluorocarbon tippet to the Copper John and around 12 inches of 5X to the dropper tied off the bend of the Copper John.

I recommend mixing in some twitches while the flies are floating downriver. The dying stoneflies will squirm around while trying to escape their entrapment in the surface film, and hoppers will be kicking their hind legs trying to reach the shore. If you are determined to fish only big dry flies, you can fish double dries with the first fly tied to the 2X and the second fly tied to around 20 inches of 2X tied off the hook bend of the first fly. Separating the flies allows you to cover more water.

## Terrestrials

The fifth group of insects that can provide dry-fly opportunities are the land-based insects collectively known as terrestrials. There are millions of different terrestrial insect species that can end up in the water and trout will eat any of them, but the groups that are important to the fly fisher include ants, beetles, and grasshoppers. They have no aquatic component (except for a few beetle species that are not significant) and spend their entire life on land, except when they inadvertently end up in the water and can provide opportunities for both trout and fly fishers. Terrestrial insects

Grasshoppers are important fish foods wherever they are found. They come in a wide array of sizes and colors.
JAY NICHOLS PHOTO

can get spooked by humans or other animals and accidentally land on the water, or they can get caught by a wind gust or just make a mistake when crawling or flying around.

Terrestrial insect activity starts in mid-spring, increases throughout the summer, and tapers off in the fall. Depending on many variables the populations of different groups or species of terrestrial insects vary year to year. In a normal year a variety of terrestrials appear on the water sporadically throughout the season, and trout feed on all of them opportunistically.

During an aquatic insect hatch, trout usually feed selectively on the hatching insect, but if you are having a problem fishing patterns matching the hatch, sometimes a beetle, ant, or hopper with an emerger dropper will work. I remember fishing the Henry's Fork in Idaho with Mike Lawson and he told me if the rising fish would not take my mayfly patterns, offer them a large Carpenter Ant. He gave me a pattern, and I hooked the first fish I cast to using the ant.

There are some years when conditions are such that some groups, most notably grasshoppers, can experience what is called an irruptive hatch, and when there is a mega hatch of hoppers massive numbers of them can be present from summer through the fall. Because of the sheer number of insects, many of them end up in the water and trout really start watching for and eating them. When a river is experiencing a "hopper year," a hopper can be a very effective pattern. Be aware that throughout the summer and fall, fish have been feeding on aquatic insects that have been hatching, and even during a hopper year I fish the HCD setup. I select dropper patterns that imitate the emergent stage of the aquatic insects that have been hatching.

Terrestrials can end up anywhere on the water's surface, but they are usually near the bank. If you see a trout sporadically rising along a bank but there is no hatch in progress, a terrestrial pattern can be an excellent choice. Although a trout may have a personal preference, most of the time they are going to feed opportunistically and a beetle, ant, or hopper can all be effective. Don't forget to give the terrestrial pattern a few twitches as it approaches the fish you saw rise.

Which pattern you choose is whatever you have the most confidence in. A well-stocked box should always have hoppers, beetles, and ants in various sizes. Personally, if I am using a terrestrial pattern it is Eric Paramore's Thunder Thighs or the BC Hopper. Trout like hoppers and hopper patterns are fun to fish, but you will hook more fish if you use the HCD setup. Ants and beetles are effective patterns and many fly fishers use them a lot, but I don't use them very often because they don't support a Copper John and a dropper very well. Tim Drummond's Tim's Beetle is a deadly beetle pattern, and a variety of red or black ant patterns can be very productive if you want to fish a single fly or with a lighter dropper.

# 2

# NYMPHS

For centuries fly anglers swung, stripped, or trolled wet flies and streamers. At some point they started fishing dry flies, but nymph fishing is a relatively new technique. It started to become a recognized discipline around the middle of the twentieth century, but it did not really take off until the 1970s. Many fly fishers today would feel severely challenged if they couldn't nymph fish, and I certainly would not want to spend a day on the water without having the option of nymph fishing. In this chapter I will offer some insight into what goes on in the world of subsurface forage and how this behavior plays a significant role in our success when nymph fishing, and discuss some nymph-fishing fundamentals.

A collection of Copper Johns tied on jig hooks, which allow the fly to ride hook point up along the bottom. LANDON MAYER PHOTO

## Fishing Nymph Combos

When I first started nymph fishing, I always fished a single fly, and that continued for many years. At some point, not sure when or why, I started to fish with two nymphs and years later often fished with three nymphs in both rivers and lakes. There is no doubt that fishing a combination of two or three nymphs increases your odds that a fish will like one of them.

Fishing two or three nymphs gives trout a choice. Some fish may prefer a particular forage species, while others prefer something different. If there is a hatch in progress, fish often feed selectively on the nymph, emergent, or adult stage of the hatching insect, but if there is not a hatch, most trout feed opportunistically. This is speculation, but I feel that even though trout will eat a variety of forage, they may have favorites that they watch for. The favored forage may be more nutritious than others, or it may just be one of the dominant species in a river or lake and is familiar and therefore readily eaten.

Fishing multiple nymphs separated by 12 to 18 inches of tippet also allows you to present the flies at different depths, which is especially significant when fishing lakes but also important in rivers. Fish will be at different sections of the water column, and you will increase the odds of a fish seeing one of the nymphs.

When setting up a nymph combo, I use different patterns depending on the time of year and where I am fishing. I like to

An angler high-sticks a nymph under an indicator in Cheesman Canyon. PAT DORSEY PHOTO

use nymphs that imitate the most available natural forage in the lake or river I am fishing, which often coordinates with what aquatic insects have been hatching. A river may have different aquatic insect species—including mayflies, midges, caddis, and stoneflies—hatching, in which case there are multiple options, but a good guideline is to use patterns representing the insects that have been most active. Of course, some rivers have important forage species, including aquatic worms, scuds, and sow bugs, that don't hatch, and in some rivers and lakes imitations of these are important when setting up a combo.

## How Nymphs Wind up in the Current

A significant part of the diet for many trout consists of immature aquatic insects. Most of the time these nymphs instinctively try to stay hidden under and in various aquatic structure so as not to get eaten, but they often end up drifting in the current, and feeding trout are always watching for them.

There are a number of reasons why nymphs end up in the current. They can inadvertently lose their grip on the bottom structure and get carried away by the current, but many end up drifting in the current due to a phenomenon called catastrophic drift. This occurs when the water volume and current forces increase or when there is a physical disruption of the bottom. Water volume can increase when there is heavy rain, during spring runoff when the snow is melting, or if dam releases are increased. Physical disruption of the bottom can occur when anglers are wading, large animals such as deer or elk walk through the water, or heavy equipment is in a river. Catastrophic drift can dislodge not only nymphs of aquatic insects, but also other aquatic fauna such as worms or scuds.

Behavioral drift is another phenomenon that can result in large numbers of nymphs drifting in the current. This occurs when aquatic insect nymphs of the same species, and often in large numbers, voluntarily let loose of their purchase and drift in the current until they find a new home. There are ideas explaining this behavior, but it is not well understood by science and further study is needed. The free-drifting nymphs are carried by the current until they are eaten or end up on some structure where they find somewhere to hide. Both catastrophic and behavioral drift result in an increased number of nymphs in the current and increased feeding activity by the trout.

Another phenomenon that increases the availability of aquatic insects to trout is when they are getting ready to hatch. Stonefly nymphs can't swim, so they leave their cover and start crawling on the bottom before exiting the water to hatch. While the nymphs crawl along the bottom, trout can pick them off, and some lose their grip and get carried away by the current, where they drift helplessly and often get gobbled up by trout. When mayfly nymphs are ready to hatch, they leave their cover and start swimming towards the surface. They are weak swimmers and, if they ascend in a strong current, they will helplessly get carried downstream until they regain control and continue the ascent to the surface. While they are drifting downstream they are easy pickings for trout.

The Copper John is my go-to generic nymph pattern. It works wonders under a dry fly, under an indicator, or tight-lined in a Euro nymphing rig. JAKE BURLESON PHOTO

When midge and caddis pupae are getting ready to hatch, they leave their protective sheath and the current carries them downstream as they swim towards the surface, making them an easy meal for a trout.

Whether due to catastrophic or behavioral drift or the aquatic insects being exposed while preparing to hatch, the increased availability of the nymphs increases feeding activity, and when trout are actively feeding, nymph fishing is better. During catastrophic drifting a variety of forage is available to trout, and they will usually feed opportunistically. A variety of nymph patterns will work, but imitating the predominant forage in a river is a good bet. Knowledge of when a hatch is likely to occur is very helpful when choosing patterns to nymph fish before the hatch. You just have get lucky to encounter a behavioral drift while fishing because they are impossible to predict and they often occur at night.

The bottom line is the more nymphs that are available to trout, the greater the

Euro fishing a deep riffle.
PAT DORSEY PHOTO

feeding activity and the better the fishing. We have all heard anglers say that the fishing "really turned on." Usually when nymph fishing noticeably improves, it is due to an increase in the available subsurface forage as a result of catastrophic or behavioral drift, or increased nymphal activity just prior to hatching.

## Nymph Fishing with an Indicator

Nymph fishing as we now know it did not arrive on the scene until the early 1970s. During the early development of nymphing techniques, fly fishers did not use indicators but watched their leader and line for a signal that a fish had taken their nymph. When I first started fishing nymphs I used a section of fluorescent monofilament for my butt section to detect strikes. That approach still works well in pocketwater and runs where the casts and drifts are short and you are high-sticking on a short line. The basic principles of that technique have morphed into the popular and deadly method that today is referred to as the Euro technique. I don't have a lot of experience with this technique's tackle and tactics, but my friend and fishing companion Jim Auman does, and he contributes his thoughts about getting started in this chapter.

When I nymph, I prefer to fish nymphs underneath a floating fly or an indicator. My first exposure to indicator nymphing was on the Deckers stretch of the South Platte River in the late '70s. I was watching an angler fishing a run with a fly rod, and he appeared to be casting a bobber. At the time I had used bobbers only when fishing

bait in stillwaters. Periodically he would rip up his rod tip and hook a trout.

I walked down to the river and asked him what he was doing. He explained that he was fishing a nymph under an indicator with a split shot pinched to the leader above the fly to sink it, and he used the indicator to detect strikes. The homemade indicator was a small cork painted fluorescent red with a hole drilled through the middle. The leader was threaded through the hole and pegged in place with a toothpick, and the split shot and nymph were attached to the tippet below the indicator.

He gave me one of his indicators and some toothpicks, and I set up my first nymph rig using an indicator. I used the same setup with the fluorescent red butt section, 5X tippet, split shot, and the fly I had been using (Polly Rosborough's Black Drake nymph) except I pegged the cork to my leader above the fly at the approximate depth of the run I was fishing. After a little practice I was able to lob it into a run and get a good drift. I will never forget the first trout I hooked and how much fun it was watching the red cork drift down the river and setting up tight into a trout when the cork twitched. I can still picture the 12-inch rainbow in my hand, but had no idea how fishing with an indicator would change how fly fishers nymph fished in the years to come.

I still enjoy nymph fishing with an indicator. Watching for the twitch and setting up tight into a trout never gets old. For many years I used homemade cork indicators that I painted fluorescent red pegged with a toothpick. Then yarn indicators came on the scene and became popular and I used those, and then many types of bobber-style

# Cranefly Larva

- **Hook:** #8-12 TMC 200R
- **Thread:** Olive 140-denier UTC Ultra Thread
- **Tail:** Clipped olive marabou
- **Body:** Olive Arizona Synthetic Dubbing
- **Back:** Black/tan Fly Specks Thin Skin
- **Notes:** This is one of the most overlooked nymph patterns for trout in lakes or rivers. My original pattern has been improved by adding a strip of Fly Specks Thin Skin for a back. The fly looks and works better than the original. I also added sizes 10 and 12, which can cross over as a large free-living caddis larva.

This quality brown ate a Cranefly Larva pattern in a South Park reservoir in Colorado. I first fished Cranefly Larva patterns in some lakes in Montana and Idaho and was amazed at how effective it was. Lakes don't have natural craneflies but many have scuds, and maybe some trout think it is a giant scud or just looks like something that might be good to eat. It's possibly the most overlooked nymph pattern in both rivers and lakes. JAY NICHOLS PHOTO

indicators came on the market and today I use a variety of those.

Nymph fishing with an indicator is highly effective and allows you to fish a wide variety of water conditions with short to long casts. All types of indicators work, and I recommend using whatever style you like. You just want it to float and be visible and adjustable. I like to use the smallest indicator that will support the weight under it because a smaller indicator is more sensitive and easier to cast. When a trout takes a nymph the indicator can get ripped under the surface, but usually it just hesitates or twitches, sometimes almost imperceptibly, and a smaller indicator is more likely to signal a subtle take. Most nymphs live and drift on or near the bottom, and we usually want to fish our flies near the bottom. Fish can be suspended anywhere in the water column and will move up or down to take food, but they usually hold near the bottom, waiting for food to be carried to them by the current.

The standard setup for nymph fishing is an indicator with one, two, or three flies below the indicator. Many of the nymphs we fish are relatively small and unweighted, and even patterns that are weighted may not provide enough weight to quickly get the flies into the productive zone near the bottom, so split shot or moldable metallic putty is added to the leader above the nymphs to sink them. I prefer to use at least one weighed nymph in my setup to sink the flies and not add split shot or putty if the water isn't too deep or the current too heavy. Eliminating the added weight makes the setup less prone to tangling while casting, and also the weight may alarm heavily pressured fish.

The nymph rig is cast into the river and the angler watches the indicator as it is drifting, and if it twitches or gets yanked under, you set the hook. The hook is set with a quick snap or sweep of the rod. The rod movement can travel on any plane from horizontal to vertical and anywhere in between. You can set forehand or backhand, whatever it takes to drive home the steel.

The traditional nymph-fishing technique is to dead drift your nymph rig, and mend the line if the indicator and nymphs are getting dragged downstream in an unnatural manner. Drag occurs when the current where the line is floating is faster than where the indicator is drifting. To prevent the line from dragging your nymphs, you either mend the line upstream of the indicator or lift the line off the water by raising your rod tip, or a combination of both. Depending on the nature of the current your rod position can change throughout the drift, but if the current is uniform, it is less wear and tear on your arm and shoulder if you keep the rod in a comfortable position and not way up in the air.

My standard presentation while drifting nymphs under an indicator is to use a combination of dead drifting and twitches, which gives the flies a little movement. Keep in mind that natural nymphs periodically swim and wriggle around as they drift, and having your nymphs move periodically while they are drifting can trigger a take. Having your indicator drag your nymphs downstream is not a natural movement. I create the twitches with a combination of rod tip movement and short strips of the line, and let the nymphs dead drift between twitches. There is no set rule on how often or how vigorously I twitch the flies, just whatever feels right.

Most fly fishers have hooked fish at the end of a drift when holding the indicator in the current while deciding where to place the next cast, but more often the cast is made as soon as the drift ends. As the flies are straightening out, don't immediately recast—instead hold them in the current for a short time and let the flies rise up. Trout will sometimes grab a rising nymph, especially if the fly is a pupa or an emerger.

Most often when nymph fishing we blind-fish water that we think holds trout—which, of course, is an effective way to fish—but to increase the odds of hooking fish an angler should always be looking for fish. If you can see a fish, drifting your nymph right to it increases the odds of success exponentially over just blind-fishing the water. If you see a fish, you want to position yourself so

that you can get a good presentation and place your cast far enough above the fish so the nymphs are at the fish's level when they reach it.

You make the cast and then watch the fish. The inside of a fish's mouth is white, and when a fish opens its mouth to take the fly, you may see this white color. Because of the angle where you are standing you may not see the white, but the fish will usually move as it takes the fly. When your fly reaches the fish, if you see a white mouth or if the fish moves, you set the hook. A fish may move to check out your fly and not take it, but any movement should be interpreted as a take and you should set.

You can sight-fish with or without an indicator, but throughout the day I am switching back and forth between blind- and sight-fishing, and I just leave the indicator attached the entire time. If I can clearly see the fish, I will make a cast and watch the fish for a white mouth or movement. If I cannot clearly see the fish, I will make the cast and glance back and forth between the fish and the indicator.

When getting ready to nymph-fish a run, the first thing you do is select the flies and tippet you want to use and tie them on. You want the flies drifting near the bottom, so you have to decide how much weight (if any) besides your flies should be added to the leader.

Next you have to ascertain the depth of the run and decide where to attach your indicator so that the flies will drift near the bottom. All you can do is make your best

Showing proper rod position while following the flies downstream with the rod tip. JAKE BURLESON PHOTO

guess as to where to set the indicator and how much weight to add, and after a few drifts you can make adjustments. If you hang up on the bottom early in the drift, remove weight or lower your indicator or do both. If you do not hang up at all or you get no signal from your indicator that you are occasionally tapping the bottom, add weight or raise your indicator or do both. The good news is that no matter where the indicator is placed and how much weight is used you will catch fish, but to optimize the chances of hooking fish your flies should be near the bottom for as much of the drift as possible.

Besides the depth, the current speed is an important consideration because the faster it is, the more weight is needed, which is especially important if the drift is fairly short. If the current is slow and the drift fairly long, the amount of weight is not as critical. The bottom line is throughout the drift you want the flies to be near the bottom for as much of the drift as possible. In a normal day we will fish a variety of water, and a good nymph fisher will adjust the indicator and weight throughout the day to accommodate the varying depths and current speeds.

When the nymphs or weight are tapping the bottom it can look like a strike, so just set and if you don't hook up just continue the drift. Many times I have fished a good-looking run without having any success, and after adding more weight or raising my indicator I started hooking fish. My flies were just not getting down to where the fish were holding. Don't forget to regularly check your flies to make sure they haven't picked up any vegetation during the drift.

## Nymph Rig Setups

I do the majority of my nymph fishing with a fast-action 9-foot 4-weight rod, a WF floating line with a 7½-foot leader tapered to 2X, and then add tippet and flies. I always use fluorocarbon tippet and usually fish three flies. How I rig the flies and tippet depends on the water conditions and what flies I am using, but the first tippet section is always 3X, which is attached to the 2X leader with a five-turn blood knot. When rigging the flies I usually like to step down the tippet size to each fly so they turn over better during the cast. If I tie the first fly to the 3X, I will tie a section of 4X to the hook bend of the first fly and tie the second fly to the 4X, and add a section of 5X tied off the hook bend of the second fly and tie on the third fly. I use a five-turn clinch knot when attaching the tippet to the hook bend and when tying on the flies.

This is my standard setup, but it can vary. I may elect to add a section of 4X to the 3X and tie on the first fly. My second fly will then be tied to 5X and the third fly to 5X or 6X depending on the conditions and fly pattern. The tippet length to each fly can vary, but it is usually around 14 to 18 inches.

Most often my first fly is a Copper John, which is both an attractor and heavy and hydrodynamic, which helps sink the flies below it if they are unweighted. It also catches fish. The flies below the Copper John are patterns representing what I think the fish may be feeding on, which often correlates with the aquatic insect activity at the time. Always keep in mind that unless there is a hatch, trout usually feed opportunistically and a wide variety of nymph patterns

Graphic Caddis. LANDON MAYER PHOTO

will work. If insects have been hatching, there are certain combos that I like.

If there has been PMD activity, I like a size 16 red Copper John with two PMD Barr Emergers for the second fly and third fly. I will use two different versions of the emerger, including the plain, flashback, or bead head, depending on what feels right. I may use one emerger and a third fly representing another insect that has been hatching or a pattern imitating a predominant forage in the river, such as a worm.

If darker caddis have been hatching, I like a chartreuse Copper John with a green Graphic Caddis Pupa for the second and sometime the third fly. If PMDs or *Baetis* have been hatching, the third fly might be a Barr Emerger imitating those insects or a pattern representing another forage found in the river. If tan caddis have been hatching, I like a standard copper-colored Copper John and a tan Graphic Caddis as the second and third fly, but there are many other options for the third fly. In some fisheries

**69**

there is a dominant forage that trout feed on year-round such as midges, scuds, sow bugs, or aquatic worms, in which case a pattern representing this forage should always be included in your setup.

## Euro Nymphing

Modern-day nymph fishing has greatly evolved since the '70s, and today there are countless ways to rig nymph setups and techniques to fish them. The most notable technique used to nymph fish is the relatively new European, or Euro, technique. I have only recently begun to learn this incredibly effective technique and have found it not only productive but a very enjoyable way to fish nymphs, but at this point my skill level is not very high. I often fish with Jim Auman from Windsor, Colorado, who is an elite fly fisher, and over the past few years he has fished the Euro technique almost exclusively. During that time he has read extensively and watched countless videos on Euro fishing, and has spent over 200 days a year on the water perfecting the technique.

Watching Jimmy cast a Euro setup is almost like watching a conductor direct a symphony, except he is slowly and gracefully moving a fly rod instead of a baton. When his flies are in the river he quietly follows them downstream with his rod tip with no mending, all the while laser focused on his sighter (indicator). When the sighter signals a take, even the set is just a gentle lift. It is boggling how he consistently hooks huge numbers of fish and in all types of water from the obscure to the defined runs.

There have been videos and much written about Euro nymph-fishing techniques, and I recommend watching the videos and reading what experts on the subject have written and then fishing with someone who is an accomplished Euro-style fly fisher. The good news is all of the setups and different techniques work, and you just need to find which one you enjoy and what works best for you and go fishing.

### EURO NYMPHING BASICS
*by Jim Auman*

I remember when Gore-Tex waders came out. When fluorocarbon tippet first hit the market. When the Barr Emerger fundamentally changed fishing for me and thousands of other anglers. In more than three decades of fishing, I've seen many new and revolutionary products introduced, but I can't recall a time when I've been more excited about learning a new method of presenting the fly than when I started Euro nymphing. This technique is certainly not new in the world of fly fishing, but it's quickly becoming more popular in America as people realize how extremely productive and nuanced Euro nymphing can be.

The rods are specifically designed for Euro nymphing, allowing an angler to fish long, light leaders with fine tippets and varying weights of flies. And while you can use your standard trout rod (9-foot 5-weight or 6-weight), Euro-specific rods that are 10 feet or longer for 2- and 3-weight lines are best suited for this casting technique.

My favorite leader is a 12-foot section of 4X sighter material and about 6 feet of 6X tippet to a two-fly rig. The sighter material is a two-tone monofilament that allows you to see the leader during the drift. The tippet is tied off of the 4X with a tippet ring. About

4 to 6 feet of tippet is added to that. Many leader formulas are available, and I would recommend starting with a slightly thicker leader. As you become comfortable casting, you can fish thinner and thinner formulas.

At the end of the 6X, I fish one or two jigged flies ranging in size from 12 to 18 and tungsten beads in sizes 2 to 4 mm. This system does not require split shot or strike indicators. Adjusting depth is achieved by changing the angle of your presentation and the weight of the fly depending on the river's depth and current speed.

The idea is to dead drift your flies with contact. That means you are not pulling your flies through the drift but leading your flies with slight tension. While your flies are drifting, watch for any movement or hesitation in the sighter. I see most of the takes and try to teach other anglers not to rely on feel but to watch for movement.

Eliminating the indicator and split shot allows you to fish varying depths and currents. Instead of finding yourself fishing the same lies and holes, now you can fish every part of the river. Pocketwater, riffles, and runs can all be fished with the same setup. Just by changing the drift angles and weights of your flies, you can move about the river and catch fish everywhere. This method allows you to fish water you never even thought of fishing before. I'm still amazed at the number of trout I was passing by before learning how to Euro nymph effectively.

Streamer fishing is another way the Euro setup shines. I use the same leader as nymphing and just tie on a small jigged streamer. This is effective because you can jig the streamer as you make drifts through any type of water. By making an upstream cast, as you would nymphing, you then lightly jig the streamer as it drifts through the current. The strikes can be violent as the streamer tumbles and jigs downstream. At the end of the drift, just swing the fly and watch the sighter. This method is also deadly in winter when the trout are grouped up in deep pools and runs.

Many anglers new to the Euro game think that dry-fly fishing is not something that can be done with this method. This is far from the truth. One of my favorite ways to fish during a hatch is to fish a dry-dropper. The Euro dry flies that I use are mostly tied with CDC (cul de canard). This type of fly floats low in the surface film and is buoyant enough to suspend a small jig-fly dropper. The style works well in smooth, glassy runs or long, flat water. I still use the same leader I use for my nymphing setup but add the dry to the top tag and use smaller 2 mm jig flies that won't drag the dry underwater. This is also a go-to rig for slow winter water when fish are feeding on midges in large pods. Winter, spring, summer, or fall, this is the way to quickly rig your Euro nymph setup to a dry-dropper.

A big misconception about Euro nymphing is that it is only effective in fast pocketwater and steep-gradient, fast-moving rivers. This is not the case at all. I have used this method in all sorts of rivers: tailwaters, freestones, and even small spring creeks are all perfect settings for Euro nymphing. Learning to use different strategies within the Euro style opens up new fishing opportunities on your favorite rivers and boosts confidence when stepping into new water. It will change the way you look at and fish a river.

I have spent countless hours reading and watching Euro nymphing lessons. If you're interested in digging deeper into the technique, I would recommend Devin Olsen's book *Tactical Nymphing.* Olsen also partners with Lance Egan to produce Euro nymphing videos that are for sale on Vimeo. I would encourage anyone interested in fly fishing to give Euro nymphing a try. It might just change your fishing game.

*Jim Auman lives in Fort Collins, Colorado, with his wife, Katie. He is an avid fly tier and lifelong fly fisher, having guided extensively in Colorado and Alaska, and spent many years working in fly shops.*

Colored leader sections are used when Euro nymphing. Master Euro nymph fisher Jimmy Auman fighting a nice brown hooked while using the Euro technique. Note the severe bend in the 10-foot 3-weight rod used with the technique. The rod allows the angler to fish the technique properly but also protects the light tippets that are used.

# TIPPET AND KNOTS

Knot failure is incredibly frustrating and totally avoidable. Most of us tie a bad knot because we are just not paying close enough attention or are in a hurry to get back to fishing. There is no excuse for not paying attention when there is no urgency, but we have to consciously force ourselves to tie a good knot under pressure. Pressure situations include tying on a fly during a hatch when the light is running out, or tying on a fly when a

school of bonefish or permit is rapidly approaching. We have to make sure that our knots are always well tied, especially when we are most likely to tie a bad one. It is bad enough to break off a fish due to something unavoidable, but the worst feeling is after "breaking off" a fish you find the dreaded ugly curlicue at the end

Learn to tie a few basic knots and practice them in the off-season until tying them on the water becomes automatic. JAKE BURLESON PHOTO

of the remaining tippet material where your barrel or clinch knot came undone.

When fly fishing for both warm- and coldwater species in freshwater, I use three knots. I use a Tie-Fast tool to make a five-turn nail knot when attaching my backing and leader to the fly line, a five-turn blood knot to attach tippet material to the leader and to join sections of tippet, and a five-turn clinch knot to attach the fly.

Other knots work well, but the important thing is to tie the knots you choose to use perfectly every time. We all know that a poorly tied knot often results in a lost fish. Probably the number one cause of knot failure is not completely seating the knot. Be sure to lubricate it with saliva before seating it. Monofilament or fluorocarbon that is lubricated will more easily slide into a good, tight knot than if it is dry. After tying the knot, examine it to see if it looks like it is seated and then test it by pulling on it and giving it a few light jerks.

A note here about tippet: The tippet you use might be more important than your fly pattern and technique. As a general rule, when fishing dry flies and nymphs I use the lightest tippet I feel comfortable with and when fishing streamers I usually fish 0X or 1X. I think trout must scrutinize nymphs and dries more so than streamers, because even for pressured fish I generally have not had a problem getting streamer takes on heavy tippets.

When choosing tippet material, your options are regular monofilament or fluorocarbon. Fluoro has two significant advantages over regular monofilament: it is less visible to the fish and has greater abrasion resistance. Fluorocarbon does sink and many anglers do not consider using it when dry-fly fishing; however, 5X and lighter fluorocarbon tippets tend not to break the surface film and work well for dry flies. When fishing small flies to large trout rising in clear, flat water the decreased visibility of the fluorocarbon is a significant advantage, and when playing large fish on light tippet the increased abrasion resistance helps prevent break-offs due to sharp teeth or structure in the water. I use fluorocarbon tippet material 100 percent of the time when fishing nymphs and streamers, and for dry flies when using 5X and lighter. When dry-fly fishing with 4X and heavier tippet, I use regular monofilament.

It has been said that fluorocarbon takes forever to break down in the environment so it should not be used, and to be environmentally responsible only regular monofilament should be used because it degrades quickly. The reality is that even though fluorocarbon is estimated to take 1,000-plus years to degrade, regular monofilament still takes 500-plus years to degrade, so you can use whichever tippet material you choose with a clear conscience, but be sure to discard all tippet in the trash.

# 3

# THE HOPPER-COPPER-DROPPER

In the early 1990s Jackson Streit, owner of Breckenridge Anglers in Breckenridge, Colorado, took me on a float trip on the Colorado River and introduced me to a technique he called the hopper-dropper, which I had never heard of or fished. He was using a buoyant hopper pattern with a tippet tied off the hook bend of the hopper and attached to a weighted nymph, a Hare's Ear as I recall. He was catching fish on both flies, with the hopper acting as an indicator when a fish took the nymph. I fished the technique the rest of the day and found it to be much more enjoyable than casting a nymph rig, and plenty of fish took the hopper. It was a fun and effective way to fish, but at the time I had no idea what an impact Jackson introducing me to the new technique would have.

Fishing the HCD rig and covering all of the water from the far bank to the near bank while Landon Mayer observes. Trout can be holding and feeding almost anywhere in a riffle. With the HCD technique it is easier to make long casts, get longer drifts, and cover more water than with an indicator or Euro nymph rig. You can also sidecast under branches and fish the far bank with greater ease. JAY NICHOLS PHOTO

After the trip I started thinking that it was a really fun and productive technique, but maybe it could be modified to be even more effective. I thought about dropping two flies below the hopper. At the time, many of the effective patterns we were using in nymph rigs were small, unweighted patterns such as emergers, pupas, and midge larvas, but split shot was required to sink the flies. The small flies fished under the hopper wouldn't have the sink rate to be effective, but if a heavy fly was tied to a tippet from the hopper and a small fly was attached to a short tippet tied to the heavy fly, it might have potential.

I began thinking about designing a fly that would hopefully catch fish but also have a rapid sink rate in order to deliver the small flies down to the trout. In addition to sinking rapidly, the fly needed to have attractive qualities to get the trout's attention so they would see the smaller, less visible fly tied on a short tippet off of the hook bend of the heavier fly. There were many weighted nymphs out there, but none of them had all of the features that I had in mind, plus I wanted to build a "better mousetrap."

This led to the development of the Copper John, which became an essential part of a new system that I was developing, which would later become the Hopper-Copper-Dropper (HCD) technique. I developed the technique years ago, and over time it has gained popularity and more and more fly fishers are using it. It consists of a hopper pattern, a Copper John tied to a tippet off the bend of the hopper, and a nymph pattern as a dropper tied off the bend of the Copper John.

The original pattern designed for the HCD was the BC (Barr/Craven) Hopper. It's being tied on here with a five-turn clinch knot. JAKE BURLESON PHOTO

To effectively fish the HCD technique the dry fly must be highly visible in all light conditions and very buoyant. That's why I use the Thunder Thighs hopper in addition to the BC Hopper. JAKE BURLESON PHOTO

A number of techniques work well when fishing nymphs, including using an indicator, high-sticking without an indicator, and the relatively new and increasingly popular Euro technique. All are effective, but the HCD technique is the most versatile, the easiest to cast, and the only one that gives fish the option of eating a dry fly. The technique is very effective and an enjoyable way to blind-fish both a dry fly and nymphs at the same time. One doesn't have to decide whether to blind-fish a dry fly or nymph-fish. The combo is fished just like you would blind-fish a dry fly, but the hopper also serves as an indicator when a fish takes the Copper or the dropper. The Copper John sinks rapidly, catches fish, and is an attractor, which enables fish to see a small dropper that they otherwise might not see.

The hopper must be very buoyant and have good visibility because it acts as a strike indicator when a fish takes the Copper John or the dropper, and the angler must be able to easily see the hopper throughout the drift. The fly must be able to support the fairly heavy Copper John throughout a long drift, and it needs to float high in the water. It must be easy to see as it floats through sunny riffles or in the shade and when a long cast is made. I always use a hopper, thus the *H*, but any of the large, buoyant, foam-bodied patterns that have a topping of hi-vis poly work just fine. My favorite hopper patterns are the BC Hopper and Paramore's Thunder Thighs. They are not only very buoyant and visible but are also effective patterns in their own right. I usually use sizes 8 to 12 but may use a 14 if conditions

When fishing the HCD setup you never know which fly a particular fish will take. I like to hook fish on the Copper or the dropper, but it is always a special thrill when you get a hopper eat. JAKE BURLESON PHOTO

This grass carp took the hopper when an HCD rig was cast well in front of the cruising carp and left motionless. Grass carp are spooky so the flies can't land too close, and the direction they cruise in is not predictable, but if you are lucky enough to hook one they will give you a ride. JAKE BURLESON PHOTO

are demanding, such as low, clear water. I like yellow- or tan-bodied patterns, but any color is fine.

When fishing the HCD technique I like to use a fast-action 9-foot 4-weight rod, but a 5-weight rod also works well. Having the right line and leader setup is very important. Not having the right setup will result in frequent tangles while casting, which will make fishing the technique rather unenjoyable. I use a WF floating line with a head that is heavily weighted towards the front of

the taper, which helps to quickly load the rod and aids in casting and turning over the flies. I always use a 7½-foot monofilament leader tapered to 2X (2X fluorocarbon will sink the hopper). I used to use a 7½-foot 3X leader but found the 2X leader turned the flies over better and was easier to cast, and plenty of fish still ate the hopper.

Depending on the depth of the water I use from 1 to 4 feet of 4X fluorocarbon tied off the hook bend of the hopper to the Copper John. I use a 4X tippet to the Copper

John most of the time but may use 5X if conditions are demanding, such as slow, clear water and bright sun, but 5X doesn't turn over as well as 4X and tangles are more likely. Most often the tippet is around 3 feet, but I will shorten it if the water is shallow and lengthen it if the water is deeper. I then use 8 to 12 inches of 5X fluorocarbon tied off the hook bend of the Copper John to the dropper. I usually use 5X to the dropper, but in extremely demanding conditions such as shallow, slow water and bright sun I may use 6X to the dropper. Stepping the leader and tippets down from 2X to 4X and 5X aids in a clean turnover of the flies. I use a five-turn clinch knot for all of the connections.

The fish will almost always see the hopper as it drifts downstream, especially if a few twitches are used. A really fun part of the technique is you can get the thrill of a hopper eat, which is always a great visual moment, but if they don't eat the hopper, the fish are looking up at the hopper as it floats down and will easily see the Copper John and dropper, which they might have missed if they weren't looking up. A fish that may be reluctant to eat the hopper will often take the Copper John or dropper without hesitation.

It is obvious when a fish takes the hopper, but you must stay laser focused on the hopper to detect when a fish takes one of the nymphs. As the hopper floats downstream, if there is any unnatural movement during the drift, that could signal that a fish has taken one of the nymphs. If a fish takes one of the nymphs the hopper may pause, twitch, or sometimes get pulled under, at which point you set up. I used to always fish the combo with a dead drift, but now, if the current allows, I frequently incorporate a few little twitches to the hopper during the drift with the rod tip or little jerks on the line. When hoppers end up in the water they start kicking with their rear legs while trying to reach the shore, and aquatic insects and other trout forage such as worms and scuds squirm and wiggle while drifting downstream.

When blind-fishing in mid-spring through fall, if I am not fishing to rising fish, I am usually fishing the HCD technique. Some years conditions result in a massive hopper hatch with many ending up in the water, and trout are really watching for them and eating them. More often, however, there are not large numbers of hoppers in the water and for whatever reason even though a trout sees a hopper, it may be reluctant to eat it. I have thrown real hoppers in rivers and they floated and kicked their way downstream and were not touched, then I floated the HCD combo through the same run and took fish on the Copper John or the dropper. The hopper will usually get the trout's attention and they will sometimes take it, but many trout are more comfortable feeding subsurface and will take the Copper or the dropper.

Trout behavior varies throughout the day and from day to day. There may be a hopper bite all day or just in the morning or the afternoon. Some days there are no hopper eats and all of the fish are hooked subsurface. Fishing the HCD technique covers all of the bases, but I never want to miss out on the thrill of a hopper eat.

The HCD technique can be fished anywhere in a run, but it is especially well suited to fishing shallow to medium-depth riffles. A significant amount of forage lives

# THE COPPER JOHN

In the early developmental stages of the Copper John there were design, material, and hook model changes. I had yet to fish any of the patterns because I didn't really like any of them. Finally I came up with a pattern that had "the look" that I had in mind. The pattern I liked suggested a mayfly or stonefly nymph, would sink rapidly, and had attractive qualities. The prototype had natural-colored brown partridge fibers for the tail, natural-colored copper wire for the abdomen, a peacock hurl thorax with partridge legs on either side of the thorax, and an epoxied turkey quill wing case. There were lead wire wraps under the thorax, and it was finished off with a gold bead. The copper wire, the lead, and the bead gave the fly a good sink rate, and the copper wire and the bead had good attractive qualities.

The idea to use copper wire for the abdomen came from my early nymph-fishing experiences. In the late 1970s I was fishing the South Platte River in the Deckers area in Colorado and ran into a gentleman who was catching a lot of fish. He showed me the pattern he was using, and he called it the South Platte Brassie. His fly was nothing but a hook shank wrapped with copper wire without a tail, thorax, or legs. No thread was used, just like the original Pheasant Tail tied by Frank Sawyer. It didn't resemble any fly I had ever seen, but it sure was effective. Of course, when I got home that night, I had to tie some Brassies. I didn't have any bare copper wire, but I did have some electrical wire that had copper wire inside the plastic coating. After removing the coating, I had a nice piece of bright, shiny copper wire.

Rows of Copper Johns, any of which are a good choice when setting up an HCD or nymph rig. Use whatever colors look good to you. JAKE BURLESON PHOTO

The Copper John in life, and art. LANDON MAYER PHOTO

I went back to the river with a box of Brassies in different sizes and proceeded to hook many fish. In a fairly short amount of time, however, the wire started oxidizing and losing its brilliance. Although the flies with the dull-colored copper wire caught fish, they were not nearly as effective as those tied with the bright, shiny copper. I went to a fly shop and found some copper wire on a spool, but the wire was in various stages of oxidation. My solution to the oxidation problem was to use an emery board on the dulled surface of the wire to restore the luster. I tried coating the wire with head cement but that did not work very well, so when I was on the water I just carried an emery board with me in order to keep the Brassies shiny.

At the time I was developing the prototype fly the tarnishing problem with the copper wire still existed, and I felt strongly that the abdomen had to have a bright, new penny appearance to produce the highly visible and attractive qualities that I wanted. I still carried an emery board to keep the wire shiny, but that was impractical. I had no solution, and the development of the pattern stalled. During this time, as luck would have it, Wapsi introduced Ultra Wire, which was an incredible breakthrough, not just for the pattern but for all fly tiers. The wire did not oxidize and tarnish, and it kept its bright sheen. It came in a natural copper color in a variety of sizes that accommodated different-sized hooks. The tarnishing problem was solved. After the initial introduction of the natural copper color many more colors were introduced, and today there is every color a tier would ever want.

The second significant breakthrough also came from Wapsi, when they introduced a synthetic vinyl material called Thin Skin, which came in a variety of colors and patterns including the same markings as turkey quill. Until the advent of Thin Skin I had used a section of natural turkey quill pulled over the thorax and coated with epoxy, but there were drawbacks to the turkey quill: it was a natural material and not readily available, it was difficult to handle on the smaller patterns, and it required two coats of epoxy to get a nice result. The first coat would soak into the quill and it needed time to set up, and a second application was needed to get a nice sheen. The Thin Skin could be cut to any width to accommodate flies down to the smallest sizes, and one coat of epoxy gave it a nice, finished appearance. It is the perfect material for wing cases and backing for scuds, sow bugs, and cranefly and caddis larvas.

One of America's finest artists, Dave Hall, suggested pulling a single strand of pearl Flashabou over the top of the Thin Skin before applying the epoxy. It really looked good and gave the fly some added pop. I used Hungarian partridge for the tails and legs of the prototypes because it looked so good, but it proved to be not very durable and was not readily available. I went to goose biots for the tail and hen saddle patch fibers for the legs. The thorax on the original pattern was peacock herl, which had become increasingly difficult to obtain and was replaced by peacock Arizona Synthetic Dubbing. The pattern was just as effective with the dubbing without the problems obtaining peacock herl.

The fly was given the name Copper John by the great Bruce Olson, who at the time was the new flies manager at Umpqua. Sadly, Bruce has passed away. Originally I designed the fly as a purpose pattern, but I was pleasantly surprised that it was as effective and at times more effective than the small dropper. The "purpose pattern" eventually morphed into a mainstream pattern on both flowing and still waters.

New variations of the Copper John: Purple, Pheasant Tail, Jig, and Steelhead. Purple-colored wire became available only recently, and trout love the color purple so I had to add the color. A variation of Sawyer's iconic Pheasant Tail is a nice addition, and the jig version of the copper, red, and chartreuse colors was a natural because of the increasing popularity of nymphs tied on jig hooks. The steelhead version was an idea that people in the Fly Shop in Redding, California, came up with. It is a killer West Coast steelhead pattern and no doubt would work equally well on the Great Lakes steelhead.

# Purple Copper John

- **Hook:** #18-12 TMC 5262
- **Thread:** Purple 70- or 140-denier (depending on hook size) UTC Ultra Thread to build a smooth, tapered underbody for the wire; fly finished with purple 8/0 UNI-Thread
- **Tail:** White goose biots
- **Abdomen:** Purple UTC Ultra Wire (small or brassie depending on hook size)
- **Thorax:** Peacock Arizona Synthetic Dubbing
- **Legs:** Mottled brown hen saddle
- **Wing case:** Brown/black Gator Thin Skin with a single strand of pearl Flashabou pulled over the top, coated with UV resin or epoxy

# Pheasant Tail Copper John

- **Hook:** #18-22 TMC 5262
- **Thread:** Rusty brown 70- or 140-denier (depending on hook size) UTC Ultra Thread to build a smooth, tapered underbody for the wire; fly finished with rust brown 8/0 UNI-Thread
- **Tail:** Reddish brown goose biots
- **Abdomen:** One strand copper and one strand dark copper UTC Ultra Wire, wound together (small or brassie depending on hook size)
- **Thorax:** Peacock Arizona Synthetic Dubbing
- **Legs:** Mottled brown hen saddle
- **Wing case:** Brown/black Gator Thin Skin with a single strand of pearl Flashabou pulled over the top, coated with UV resin or epoxy

# Copper John Jig (Chartreuse)

- **Hook:** #12 Daiichi 4647
- **Bead:** Gold tungsten (3.3 mm)
- **Thread:** 6/0 Danville
- **Thorax:** Peacock herl
- **Legs:** Partridge
- **Tails:** Black stripped goose biot
- **Wing case:** Brown Thin Skin and pearl Flashabou coated with epoxy
- **Body:** Chartreuse UTC Ultra Wire

# Steelhead Copper John

- **Hook:** #10 TMC 5262
- **Bead:** Gold (3.8 mm)
- **Thread:** 6/0 Danville
- **Legs:** Partridge
- **Tails:** Black goose biots
- **Thorax:** Peacock sword
- **Wing case:** Black Thin Skin and pearl Flashabou coated with epoxy
- **Body:** Black UTC Ultra Wire (medium)
- **Legs:** White Spanflex (small)

**Above:** Visually following the hopper as the HCD rig floats downstream. I am watching for the hopper to pause, twitch, or get pulled under, which will indicate that a fish has taken the Copper or the dropper. JAY NICHOLS PHOTO

**Facing top:** Stripping in line so there is no slack between the HCD rig and my rod tip, which facilitates setting quickly if a fish takes one of the flies. Keeping the slack out of the line also allows me to twitch the hopper with the rod tip or by stripping the line. JAY NICHOLS PHOTO

**Facing bottom:** I keep the line pinched against the cork during the drift to ensure solid contact while setting the hook. JAY NICHOLS PHOTO

in the riffles, and trout that are in riffles are usually feeding and are much more likely to eat a fly than fish hanging out and resting in the deeper, slower water. Also, riffles are prime water for hopper eats.

One of my favorite parts of a run is at the upper end where the water enters it. The water can be fairly shallow and swift with a mixed gravel and rock bottom, which is prime habitat for some aquatic nymphs. If nymphs are getting active before and during a hatch, they can be easy pickings, and it is amazing how many trout will move up out of the main run and get into that shallow, fast water and feed on the vulnerable nymphs.

Don't ever think that the water is too shallow and fast to hold trout. If the lighting is favorable you can sometimes see the fish, especially if they are large, but most often you are blind-fishing. I may have 3 feet of tippet to the Copper John while fishing through the main part of a run, but when I get to the shallow head, I may shorten the tippet to 1 to 2 feet.

In early summer 2020 I was fishing a stretch of water in the Poudre River outside of Laporte, Colorado, and had some memorable moments while fishing the HCD technique. There had been sporadic hatching of PMDs and small tan caddis all morning but just an occasional rise here and there, so I opted to fish the HCD setup. Spring through fall I always carry two rods—a

4-weight rigged with the HCD setup and a 3-weight rigged for dry-fly fishing if there is a chance of finding rising fish—but there wasn't enough surface activity to justify switching rods. The HCD setup had been very productive all morning, so the dry-fly rod stayed propped up in the willows on the bank. I was using a size 12 hopper, a size 16 Copper John, and a size 18 Dark Back Emerger. The PMDs were about a size 18 and the tan caddis were small, and the Dark Back is a good pattern if the fish are feeding on the emergent stage of both insects.

My two largest fish that day came from shallow, fast water flowing over a gravel bottom before shelving into a long, deep run. I was fishing the HCD and had shortened my tippet to the Copper John to about 18 inches, with a Dark Back Emerger about 10 inches below the Copper John. The sun was behind me, so I could see into part of the water, but much of the shallow riffle was covered in shade from a tree. I was not ready for what happened on my first cast into the sunny part of the shallow riffle where I had good visibility. The combo landed and floated downstream a few seconds, and a monster trout came out of the shade and streaked towards my flies. It came 6 to 7 feet across the sunlit gravel and ate one of the nymphs. After a prolonged battle ending well downriver, a cutbow hybrid in the 7- to 9-pound category came to the net. To my surprise it ate the size 18 Dark Back, but no

**Facing top:** A run like this can hold fish anywhere, and to thoroughly cover all the water that you can reach can take several hours. If no fish are rising, it is perfect water to blind-fish with the HCD setup. The entire run can hold fish, but an especially productive zone to target is where the bottom transitions from shallow to deeper water. Fish like to hold in these transition zones. JAY NICHOLS PHOTO

**Facing bottom:** As you work your way upriver you want to make multiple casts that cover the transition zone all the way to the top of the run. JAY NICHOLS PHOTO

# Dark Back Emerger

- **Hook:** #16-20 Lightning Strike SE5
- **Thread:** Light Cahill 8/0 UNI-Thread
- **Tail:** Clipped brown hackle fibers
- **Abdomen:** Brown Super Fine dubbing
- **Thorax:** Amber Super Fine dubbing
- **Legs:** Clipped ginger hackle fibers
- **Wing case:** Black/tan Fly Specks Thin Skin

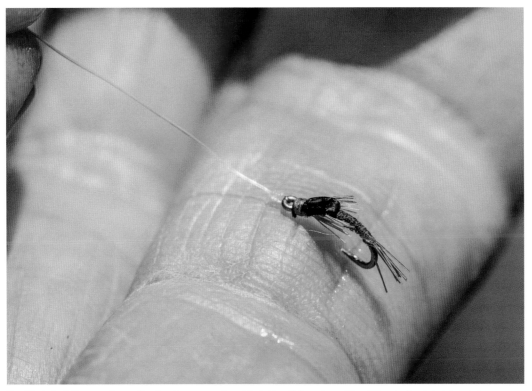

The Black Back Emerger is an effective dropper under a Vis-A-Dun if there is a midge, Trico, or *Baetis* hatch. It's also excellent as part of a nymph or HCD rig if there has been midge, Trico, or *Baetis* activity. JAKE BURLESON PHOTO

doubt what initiated the charge was the size 12 hopper floating down or a glint of sunlight off the Copper John.

The exact same scenario was repeated in the same riffle a while later. This time a 6- to 7-pound cutbow came charging out of the shadows and ate the Dark Back. The large hopper or the shiny Copper John got the cutbows' attention, but both fish ate the emerger which they couldn't have seen from that far away. No doubt the fish lived in the deep run but moved up into the shallow, fast riffle to feed on nymphs and emergent stages of the PMDs and tan caddis that were hatching.

As I mentioned, I like to use a buoyant hopper pattern such as Paramore's Thunder Thighs and almost always use a size 14 or 16 Copper John under that. The dropper can be any fly, but I usually like to use a pattern representing the nymph or emergent stage of the prevailing insect activity at the time or any pattern representing the predominant forage in a particular fishery. The hopper and Copper John are a constant, and you just need to pick an appropriate dropper depending on what insects have been hatching. In addition to patterns that imitate the nymph or emergent stage of the insects that have been hatching, good choices for the

A perfect specimen that ate a Black Back Emerger when I fished an HCD rig in the fall on the Poudre River in Colorado.

Even though dry-fly floatant has been applied to the fly, the fly will start losing its buoyancy after a number of casts and hooked fish. An occasional treatment with Shimazaki Dry-Shake is a good idea to keep a hopper or any dry fly floating high in the water. JAKE BURLESON PHOTO

dropper also include patterns imitating any of the important forage in the river you are fishing, such as worms, scuds, or sow bugs.

For example, a combo I like to use when there has been PMD activity is a size 16 red Copper John and a PMD Barr Emerger or a Dark Back Emerger dropper. The Copper John is a good imitation of the PMD nymph, and either emerger is a good imitation of the natural PMD emerger. I think that when the fly is submerged the red-colored Copper John looks more reddish brown, which is the color of many PMD nymphs, and the shape and size match up well with the natural nymph.

If there have been heavy hatches of dark caddis, such as the Black Caddis on the Big Horn River in Montana or the Mother's Day Caddis on the Arkansas River in Colorado, a deadly combo is a size 16 chartreuse Copper John with a green Graphic Caddis Pupa dropper. Don't forget to twitch the hopper periodically throughout the drift, which will also cause the Copper John and the pupa to move. Caddis pupae wriggle around as they are ascending towards the surface during hatching, and the movement will get a trout's attention.

One of my favorite all-around combos that I use throughout the season from spring through fall is a size 14 or 16 Pheasant Tail Copper John with a Black Back Emerger dropper. The Black Back Emerger is the original *Baetis* version of the Barr Emerger with a black flashback wing case. It is just a fishy pattern and can suggest a *Baetis* or Trico emerger or a midge pupa, and can trigger a take from trout that have been feeding on Trico spinners. I think that trout key on the color black when eating the spinners.

If the line, leader, and tippet setup is proper, casting the HCD combo is not much different than casting a single dry fly. The backcast should be a smooth acceleration, with a slight pause to allow the hopper and the nymphs to straighten out before smoothly accelerating a forward cast. The loop will be a bit wider and the tempo a little slower than if you were casting a single

dry fly but not that much different. After casting the HCD for a while, you will embed the timing and tempo into your memory bank and your muscle memory will allow you to enjoyably cast the combo for hours with few if any tangles.

You don't have to wait until the natural hoppers start hatching to fish the HCD technique. It is a good technique to fish in the spring before hoppers have begun to hatch. We have all had trout try to eat an indicator in the spring, and some trout will try to eat a hopper pattern before the natural hoppers have started to hatch. Even though not many fish will eat the hopper, the user-friendly technique is an easier and more pleasant way to fish nymphs than with an indicator, and it is much easier than fishing the Euro technique.

# Thunder Thighs Hopper

- **Hook:** #8-14 TMC 5262
- **Thread:** Hopper yellow UTC 140
- **Body/Leg (Bottom):** Gold Fly Foam (2mm) marked with Sharpie
- **Body/Leg (Top):** Tan Fly Foam (2mm)
- **Eye:** Black Fly Foam (2mm)
- **Indicator:** Orange Fly Foam (2mm)
- **Wing:** White Poly Yarn
- **Leg:** Tan Spanflex (small) barred black with Sharpie
- **Thorax:** Tan Buggy Nymph Dubbing

4 ———————

# THE POPPER-
# DROPPER

The focus of this book is primarily trout, but I also have
a passion for warmwater species, especially largemouth
and smallmouth bass and brim. There are many species
of brim, but where I fish the dominant species is bluegill,
though I am guessing all of the brim species have similar
behavior. I really enjoy topwater fishing for the various
species and want to share some of what I have learned
through the years that has really enhanced my topwater
success. Combos for trout are a central theme of the
book, and I have also developed a deadly topwater combo
for bass and brim that will hook far more fish than just
fishing a popper by itself.

I love casting to cruising bass in
the shallows. JAKE BURLESON PHOTO

I live in Boulder, Colorado, which is located where the foothills of the Rockies start, in the area referred to as the Front Range. When people think of Colorado they think trout, but the Front Range has hundreds of old gravel mining pits that filled with water after the mining was finished, as well as many reservoirs for water storage. Many of the reservoirs and gravel pits get too warm in the summer for trout, but most have ideal environments for warmwater species and almost every one of the bodies of water contain bass and brim as well as other warmwater species such as wipers, crappies, and carp. I have dozens of ponds and reservoirs within a short drive from my home, and over the years have spent countless hours pursuing bass and brim.

In Colorado I start warmwater fishing in late March, and with the water being cold the only viable option is to fish subsurface. In the spring the level of activity of all warmwater fish is largely dependent on water temperature, and their surface prey such as dragonflies and frogs are not around until the water warms up. The fish are therefore not looking towards the surface for food until the water warms. I always look forward to fishing top water for bass and brim, which starts sometime in the middle of May to early June depending on when the water warms up and continues through fall.

For many years when fishing top water for bass and brim I always fished a single popper—large ones for bass and small ones for brim—but at some point I started wondering how a popper-dropper combo might work and if the same combo could be used for both bass and brim. For a number of seasons I had been fishing the Hopper-Copper-Dropper (HCD) technique for trout and had found that the number of fish hooked when fishing the combo increased significantly over when fishing a hopper by itself. Trout that were reluctant to take the hopper would regularly take the Copper John or the dropper, and I started thinking that bass and brim may behave similarly when using a popper-dropper combo.

My thinking was that the popper-dropper combo would give the bass and brim the option of eating the popper or the dropper, just like the HCD technique gives trout the option of the hopper or the Copper John or dropper. I didn't want to use two flies under the popper like in the HCD technique because often I fish close to the shoreline or other structure, and one dropper fly on a short tippet would be more practical. My thinking at the time was that when a fish took the dropper, the popper would act as a strike indicator. It would be just like watching the hopper when fishing the HCD technique or the indicator when nymph fishing for trout. I would fish the popper like I always did with various retrieves and pauses, but in addition to reacting when a fish took the popper, I would set up if the popper twitched or was jerked in an unnatural manner. The technique is pretty simple and straightforward and the first time I fished the popper-dropper technique it worked just as I had envisioned, and it was a really fun technique to fish. I caught bass

**Facing:** Nice smallmouth that took the Cat while fishing the popper-dropper technique. When I fish this technique the fish have a choice. The popper always gets the bass's attention but they may be reluctant to take it, but the dropper will often get taken with no hesitation. JAKE BURLESON PHOTO

The flies I use when targeting bass and brim. If there is a subsurface bite, I feel confident that a properly presented Meat Whistle or Slumpbuster will be effective. If there is a topwater bite, I feel confident that the Cat with a Johnny Legs dropper will work. Large brim can get the larger flies in their mouth, and decent-size and bigger brim can get the Johnny Legs in their mouth. Even though I may be targeting bass, I also hook grass and common carp, wipers, and catfish on the same subsurface flies. JAKE BURLESON PHOTO

The Cat showing the high vertical white face with the undulating marabou and rabbit strip. I don't think the color of a popper is relevant to the bass, and after many years of topwater bass fishing all I carry are black Cats. The rabbit strip tail and marabou collar undulate even when the popper is sitting still, suggesting life, and this is significant because many bass take the popper when it not being retrieved. The face design allows you to subtly or aggressively pop the fly and to create a nice bow wake if slowly hand-twisted. The white face makes the popper much easier, which is important when detecting a dropper take in poor light. JAKE BURLESON PHOTO

on both the popper and dropper and blue-gill on the dropper. (The popper I use for bass is too big for all but the jumbo blues.)

My primary target is usually bass, but I am always happy when I hook a quality bluegill. Bluegill is the primary brim species in Colorado, although there are others such as green sunfish and pumpkinseed, which I catch, but the majority of the brim I catch are bluegill. I love all of the brim species because they are charismatic and are shaped and colored like fish that live around saltwater reefs, and they eat flies with tremendous enthusiasm.

In Colorado I consider a bluegill over 6 inches to be a quality fish and a fish 8 inches or larger as trophy size. Bluegills usually travel in schools that contain all sizes of fish and it is difficult to single out the bigger ones, so you never know what size fish is going to eat the dropper. Besides their appeal, if the bass bite is slow, brim are almost always on the bite and can provide good action between bass.

After finding that the technique worked, I wanted to do more field-testing and compare fishing the popper by itself versus fishing the popper-dropper combo. I regularly

# The Cat

- **Hook:** #6-10 TMC 8089
- **Thread:** Red GSP 100
- **Tail:** Black rabbit strip
- **Flash:** Blue-silver flake Holographic Flashabou
- **Collar:** Black marabou
- **Popper head:** Black deer hair
- **Face:** White deer hair

# Johnny Legs

- **Hook:** #8-10 Umpqua U555 Jig
- **Thread:** Rusty brown 140-denier UTC Ultra Thread
- **Cone:** Tungsten (medium)
- **Tail:** Rust marabou
- **Flash:** Copper Holographic Flashabou
- **Body:** Brown-yellow variegated chenille (medium)
- **Legs:** Orange/orange-black flake Speckle Flake Sili Legs

fished a couple of ponds where, if the sun was at a good angle, I could see the bass and bluegills cruising or suspended. I rigged up two rods—one with just the popper and the other with a popper-dropper combo—to see how the two different techniques compared, and spent many days fishing both the popper by itself and the combo.

In the ponds I could regularly spot fish laid up or cruising, so I had lots of targets and I could see how they reacted after I made a cast. When the popper fished by itself hit the water, the bass would immediately react. Sometimes the bass would spook but usually they would swim over and check it out as it was sitting still, and if they didn't strike I would start a retrieve. The bass might follow the popper during the retrieve and sometimes take it, but often they would just swim away. When I fished the popper-dropper combo the reaction was the same after the popper hit the water, but those that didn't take the popper almost always took the dropper soon after the popper hit the water or during the retrieve. Bluegills sometimes tried to eat the popper, although it was too large for most of them, but they always took the dropper.

A trophy bluegill (for Colorado) caught while fishing a popper-dropper combo. Both bass and brim can be caught on the combo and it is really fun to fish, because just like the HCD combo you catch fish on the nymphs with the added thrill of a dry-fly (popper) eat.

Russ Miller netting a nice smallmouth. JAKE BURLESON PHOTO

After a time I concluded that the combo was significantly more effective than the popper fished by itself. I think most fish, including bass, brim, and trout, feel more comfortable feeding subsurface than from the surface. There are times when the topwater bite is wide open and I just fish the popper, but most of the time it is not wide open and I will hook far more fish with the combo than with the single popper.

As I mentioned, the popper I use for bass is too large for most bluegills except for the real jumbos, and when fishing the combos almost all the bluegills are caught on the dropper. A bluegill-sized popper can be used if they are your primary target, and a bass will take a small popper, but I like a combo with a larger popper because it is easier to see than a small popper. I also feel more confident that the larger popper will be more appealing to bass, and although I love brim, bass are usually my primary target.

I have fished topwater bass for many years and have tried many different kinds and styles of poppers, and I have concluded that if there was a topwater bite, they all work. But after time, a popper I designed named the Cat became my confidence pattern and is now the only popper I use. It is effective and turned out to be the perfect popper to fish my new technique. All poppers will catch fish, but when fishing the popper-dropper technique the majority of your takes will be on the dropper, and to detect these takes your popper must be very visible under all light conditions, especially in poor light such as on a cloudy day or early or late in the day. The Cat sits high in the water, giving a good profile, and its white face gives it good visibility, which is very important when a take on the dropper only causes the hopper to quiver.

After trying different colors through the years I concluded that they all worked equally well, and for no particular reason I now only fish black-colored Cats. Bass are not picky when taking a popper, and carrying just one color simplifies my fly box and makes pattern selection easy. I tie the Cat on a Tiemco TMC 8089 hook in sizes 6 and 10. If you are not familiar with this hook, it has a supersized gap and a size 6 looks like a normal size 1/0 and a size 10 like a size 2.

The Cat has a clipped black deer hair body with a clipped white deer hair face, and large doll eyes. The front of the popper is vertical and fairly high so it can create a lot of surface disturbance if I am using an aggressive retrieve, or just a subtle pop when fished slowly, and it creates a nice bow wake if I am retrieving with no pops. It has a marabou collar right behind the deer hair head and a rabbit strip tail and a few strands of Holographic Flashabou. The marabou collar and rabbit undulate in the water when the fly is retrieved or sitting still, suggesting life, and the Flashabou adds

This nice smallmouth ate a size 10 Johnny Legs. JAKE BURLESON PHOTO

a little more suggestion of life. It creates a fairly high profile that, combined with the white face, makes it easy to see after it hits the water and during the retrieve.

When I first started fishing the popper-dropper combo, I wanted a dropper pattern that would not only catch bass but also be small enough that larger brim could get it in their mouth, but not so small that small brim would be constantly hooked. I love catching quality brim, and if the bass bite is slow brim can provide action between the bass.

Originally I used a dropper pattern called the Spork, which was effective, but it has been replaced by a more effective pattern that I named the Johnny Legs, which I also use for trout when setting up a nymph rig for lakes and rivers or as a trailer behind a streamer.

Any pattern can be used for the dropper, but the Johnny Legs is my confidence pattern. It is not designed to imitate any particular forage but rather is just a fishy pattern. The Johnny Legs is fairly small, about 1½ inches long, and is tied on a size 10 Umpqua U555 jig hook, which is strong and has a large gap. It has a marabou and Holographic Flashabou tail, chenille body with Sili Legs legs, and a small tungsten cone, which causes the fly to ride hook point up. The fly doesn't have to ride hook point up when used as a dropper, but I also use the Johnny Legs for carp and when fishing for carp I like to retrieve the fly on the bottom.

The larger brim can get the size 10 Johnny Legs in their mouth whereas the smaller ones have a hard time, so when you hook a bluegill on the Johnny Legs it is usually a nice one. I felt confident that smaller bass

and all sizes of brim would take the dropper, but I was not sure if larger bass would take it. At first I thought it was an aberration when a large bass would take the relatively small dropper, but after catching many adult bass on it I came to expect it, even though I still smile when I land a fish with a 4-inch-diameter mouth and a 1½-inch fly in it. Of course, if you are just targeting bass a larger "bass size" fly can be used, but I have not found that necessary since I have caught so many adult bass on the relatively small dropper fly and I don't want to miss out on a quality bluegill.

Bass and brim are very opportunistic feeders, and a number of different colors have worked well. I use a few different colors depending on the visibility of the water. In clear water I like the rust or black and olive color, and in off-colored water I like the all black or the black and olive version.

An important difference between trout and bass is how they feed. Although trout usually feed opportunistically they can still be picky, sometimes focusing on the most abundant forage, and they can become super selective during a hatch. On the other hand, bass and brim will almost always feed opportunistically and will eat pretty much anything they can capture at any time. No doubt in some fisheries some bass may key on certain prey, but I have not experienced that. I have fished for bass that were feeding on top during a *Callibaetis* hatch or a particular small mayfly that hatches in some of the ponds I fish. They were cruising along and head tailing while feeding on the mayflies, just like trout. In that scenario the trout would be feeding selectively and a pattern imitating the mayfly dun or emerger

Searching the shallows with the popper-dropper combo. I love when a bass or brim takes a popper, but I also get a thrill out of watching the popper for an indication that a fish has taken the dropper and getting tight on a dropper-hooked fish. RUSSELL MILLER PHOTO

would be required, but on different ponds where I have fished these hatches, every bass that was feeding on the mayflies took the Cat without hesitation when I dropped it in front of them.

Bass and brim are not only opportunistic feeders but usually are not leader shy like trout can be, and much heavier tippets can be used than when trout fishing. For trout 4X to 6X tippets are standard, whereas for bass and brim I use 0X and 1X. The bass and brim flies are tied on relatively large hooks compared to many of the trout flies

that are often tied on small hooks. Bass and brim can consistently provide great action throughout the season, and with the relatively large hooks you have a high-percentage hooking and landing rate and with the heavy tippets you don't have to worry about breaking fish off unless they dive into a pile of logs or branches or burrow into some heavy weeds. They are the perfect fly-rod fish.

Although most often I am blind-fishing, there is one scenario where I sight-fish for bluegill and it is when they are on their

Proper rod and line position while waiting for the fly to sink. The rod and line should be in almost a straight line with as little slack as possible so that when a fish takes the fly you can instantly strip-set. I am watching the line for a twitch or unnatural movement, which signals when a fish takes the fly. I strip-set with my left hand as hard as I can if the line looks different. Note the hi-vis floating line tip, which is needed to readily see line movement when a fish takes a fly.

spawning beds. The larger bluegills in the pond are the spawners, and you can target them when they are on the beds. They are protective of their beds and aggressive, and will readily take a fly. I use the same Cat–Johnny Legs combo that I use when blind-fishing. I cast past the targeted fish and slowly retrieve the flies so the dropper comes right in front of the fish, and it is almost a sure thing it will take it. The fish can be landed and released quickly and they immediately return to their bed, so no harm is done.

When bluegills are spawning numerous individuals form a big colony containing many beds, and there are usually some big bass staged almost motionless around the perimeter of the spawning beds waiting for

A zone that both trout and bass like to feed in is where shallow water transitions to deeper water. Crawdads and small fish are found in this zone, which is why predators like to cruise it. This is a great place for a Meat Whistle hopped along the bottom or a popper-dropper. RUSSELL MILLER PHOTO

just the right moment to explode onto the bed and try to grab one of the bluegills. When I am fishing bluegill beds I am always checking for bass lurking around the edge of the colony and have caught many quality bass while fishing the beds. I use the same combo for the bass that I do for the bluegills, and like the bluegills, almost all of the bass are caught on the dropper.

I don't sight-fish for bass on their spawning beds because if a big female is hooked the fight can last a while, and I hate thinking it might have a negative effect on her. But the reality is during spawning season when blind-fishing the perimeter of a pond you will catch bass on beds, but fortunately like the bluegills they will return to the bed after being released.

Smallmouth are somewhat chameleonlike in that they can change the color pattern on their body depending on the amount of light where they are swimming, the time of year, or when hiding in the weeds to ambush prey. This beautifully patterned smallmouth was hooked on a Meat Whistle fished along the edge of a weed bed, so it may have assumed the camouflage pattern to blend in with the weeds.

Admiring a trophy smallmouth (for Colorado). When I hooked the fish it was so strong and had such endurance, I thought I had hooked a channel cat. My jaw dropped when I first saw that I was hooked up to a monster smallmouth.

I fish the popper-dropper combo just like I fish a single popper. I make a cast and let the flies sit before starting the retrieve. It is not uncommon for a bass to take the popper or the dropper soon after the combo lands. If a bass doesn't take one of the flies after making the cast I will start retrieving them, and during the retrieve I pause frequently. While the popper is retrieved it lifts the dropper up, and during the pause the dropper sinks. Bass love to take flies that are dropping, and many bass take the dropper as it is sinking during the pause. Many fish also take the popper when it is sitting still. Just like when fishing the passive streamer technique, pausing the flies suggests prey that may be wounded and triggers the predatory instincts of the bass.

The popper-dropper can be fished with various retrieves to accommodate the conditions and whatever mood the bass are in. I fish a variety of retrieves, often during the same cast, and if the bass are responding best to a particular retrieve I will emphasize that retrieve. In low light or choppy water I usually like to pop the Cat aggressively, with the vertical face spraying some water, but always with pauses throughout the retrieve. In good light with a calm surface I like to make gentle pops with frequent pauses.

One of my favorite retrieves doesn't include any pops: I just slowly move the popper along the surface with a continuous hand twist and the popper pushes out a subtle bow wake. Sometimes I will speed up the continuous hand twist, which causes the popper to gurgle along the surface like a slow-rolled buzz bait. I still include pauses when using the continuous hand twist. Remember it is important to always let the flies sit motionless after making a cast and to include pauses no matter what retrieve is used. Many bass, including some of my largest, have been hooked when the flies are sitting still.

Small bass and most brim usually hit the dropper aggressively and the popper noticeably moves, but ironically when a big bass takes the dropper, often the popper barely moves and at times the movement is almost an undetectable quiver. This is because a big bass just inhales the dropper rather than slamming it like a smaller bass does. When the popper moves at all unnaturally I will tip-set, and if it is a big fish I follow with a few strip-sets.

I use the same rod, line, and leader whether fishing top water or subsurface: a 9-foot fast-action 6-weight rod, hi-vis WF floating line, and 7½-foot 0X leader. I use an 0X fluorocarbon tippet when fishing a Meat Whistle subsurface but a 0X regular monofilament tippet when fishing the popper-dropper combo because the fluorocarbon would sink the popper. I use around 8 to 10 inches of 0X fluorocarbon to the dropper, because when the popper lands that is where the bass's immediate focus is, and with the dropper a short distance from the popper the bass will see it. Also, bass like to hang out around structure such as logs and rocks and they like edges such as the border of a weed bed or the most dominant edge, the bank. With a short dropper tippet the flies can be landed close to these productive zones.

The visibility of the line is irrelevant when fishing top water, but I use the same setup when fishing Meat Whistles subsurface and I want the hi-vis line to help detect when a bass has taken the fly. I often carry two rods—one rigged with a Meat Whistle and one with the popper-dropper combo. Even after the water has warmed up, the topwater fishing is not always predictable and certain areas of a pond are better fished subsurface, and it is easier to just switch rods rather than re-rig the one rod. With two rods it is easy to switch tactics depending on the bite and where in the pond I am fishing.

# 5

# DROWNED SPINNERS

When most fly fishers think of mayfly spinners, their image is of a swarm of spinners dancing above the water, mating, laying eggs, dying, and producing a spinner fall with many rising trout. Spinner falls can provide excellent opportunities to fish for large rising trout, but with the exception of Tricos, being on the water when there is a spinner fall is not always predictable. Air and water temperature, clouds, sun, humidity, and factors that are not well understood play a significant role not only when and if mayflies hatch but also when they turn into spinners. The spinner falls of some species occur only at night, and some species do not produce a spinner fall because they lay their eggs subsurface and the spinners are carried downstream underwater.

The anticipation builds knowing that almost every fish in the river will be rising soon as an impressive swarm of Trico spinners gets closer to the water. COURTESY OF PAUL RUSSELL

Male Trico spinner. JAY NICHOLS PHOTO

Most spinner falls occur in rivers, with a notable exception being mayfly species in the *Callibaetis* genus that hatch and produce spinner falls in lakes. Whether the spinners are in rivers or lakes, trout love to feed on them.

At times it seems like every fish in a run is rising during a spinner fall, but they can be very difficult to fool. When trout are feeding on the motionless floating spinners, they are ultra-selective and a well-matched pattern, a dead drift, and an accurate presentation are essential. For years I experienced a lot of frustration when fishing spinner falls. There were all these rising fish and I knew what they were feeding on, but I often had a difficult time consistently hooking fish. A natural spinner floats with its body and wings flush on the surface, and the traditional approach for fishing spinner falls is to use a single floating pattern tied with spent wings and dead-drifted flush in the surface film. For many years that was how I fished spinner falls and it can be a difficult and frustrating endeavor, even for accomplished fly fishers.

My number-one problem fishing a spinner fall with a spent pattern fished in the surface film was not being able to see the fly on a consistent basis. If the lighting was not good it was often difficult to follow the pattern during the drift, and if the spinner fall was heavy the pattern could get lost in the maze of naturals. Without consistent visual contact with the fly, I would often "guess strike" if a fish rose where I thought my fly was. Sometimes I would get lucky, but usually not. If I could not clearly see the fly, it was difficult to tell if the cast was accurate or if tiny microcurrents were moving the fly in an unnatural manner, causing drag. Natural spinners are dead and motionless, and if a spinner pattern drags during the drift there is little chance that a fish will take it.

When fishing a spinner fall, my success rate compared to the number of fish feeding and the number of casts made to rising fish was not good. To compound the problem, since my success rate was generally poor, I never developed confidence in any particular spinner pattern. I was never sure if hen hackle tips or poly was the best wing material, or if the fly should have a dubbed, biot, or stripped quill abdomen. All of the patterns worked, but I never came to any definitive conclusions on which one was the most effective. I always enjoyed the adrenalin rush that casting to so many rising fish produced, but after the spinner fall ended and the feeding frenzy was over the thrill often turned to frustration because even though I had cast to many fish, I usually had limited success.

At some point I had an idea on how to fish spinner falls that might solve some of the problems I had experienced for so many years fishing a single floating spinner pattern. At the time I had been having success fishing mayfly hatches with a Vis-A-Dun and a drowned emerger dropper and wondered if a Vis-A-Dun with a drowned spinner dropper might have potential. During a spinner fall it seems like every trout is feeding on the floating naturals, but some of the spinners had to end up subsurface and no doubt trout would snap them up along with those on the surface. I also feel that trout scrutinize a floating fly more carefully than they do a submerged fly and would be more apt to take a sunken spinner pattern than a floating pattern, and that a drowned pattern would be more readily spotted by a feeding trout than a floater, especially during a heavy spinner fall.

My plan was to use a Vis-A-Dun with the same body length and color as the natural spinner so as not to alarm the trout when it floated over them, and drop a drowned spinner matching the naturals on a short tippet tied off the bend of the Vis-A-Dun. The highly visible Vis-A-Dun would allow me to monitor the drift for drag and accuracy and would serve as an indicator when a fish took the drowned spinner. The technique was worth a try, but I had no idea if it would work.

The first time I fished the combo was during a Trico spinner fall on the Missouri River in Montana. I will never forget wading into the river and getting in position to cast to a pod of fish gorging on Trico spinners. I tied on a black-bodied Vis-A-Dun that had a body the same length as the naturals to about a 24-inch piece of 6X fluorocarbon tippet. I tied around 8 inches of 6X fluorocarbon tippet to the hook bend of the Vis-A-Dun and attached a black-bodied drowned spinner pattern that matched the naturals. I picked out a rising fish and presented the flies a short distance upstream of the fish. When the flies reached the fish the Vis-A-Dun suddenly disappeared, and I set up and was tight to the fish. The quality brown instantly went airborne, and I am not sure if the fish or I was more surprised. I landed him and saw the drowned spinner buried in his lip.

During the rest of the spinner fall, if the Vis-A-Dun was pulled under or just twitched I would set up on a trout that had eaten the drowned spinner. I could easily see the

white wings on the Vis-A-Dun, which made it easy to detect when a fish took the spinner, and I was able to monitor my cast for accuracy and if any microcurrents were creating drag. After the spinner fall ended and the fish quit rising, I knew that the new technique would change forever how I fished spinner falls.

An unexpected bonus was some of the fish took the Vis-A-Dun. It had always been an effective dun pattern, but I had no idea that trout would also take it as a floating spinner. The Vis-A-Dun does not look like a traditional spent-wing pattern, but since it hooked fish it must have looked like a floating spinner to some of the trout. I feel the strongest trigger for trout feeding on spinners is the color and length of the body, and since the hackle on the Vis-A-Dun is clipped flush with the body, the body is floating in the surface film and that must have been what the trout were keying on.

From that day forward, fishing a spinner fall has been no more difficult than fishing a Vis-A-Dun and sunk-spinner dropper. I do not know how many drowned naturals a trout sees during a spinner fall, but they must see some because trout do not hesitate to snap up a well-presented sunk spinner. The spinner fall curse had at long last been lifted. In addition to Trico spinner falls, the technique works for other spinner falls as well, using patterns to match the naturals. For example, during a Rusty Spinner fall I use a Vis-A-Dun with a rust-colored body and a Drowned Rusty Spinner.

I still carry a few floating spinner patterns because sometimes the drowned spinner doesn't work well, but this doesn't happen very often. The Vis-A-Dun floating spinner combo is fished just like the combo with the sunk spinner.

Some mayflies do not produce a spinner fall but rather crawl underwater to lay their eggs. For years I wondered why species in the *Baetis* genus, which produce some of the most prolific hatches we see in the West, never produced an equally massive spinner fall. The answer is that members of the *Baetis* genus lay their eggs underwater. The female, accompanied by the male, crawls down rocks, sticks, and vegetation under the surface and lays her eggs subsurface, and when the process is finished both the male and female die. Some of the spinners will float to the surface, resulting in sporadic rises, but most remain submerged and become part of the drift that brings nymphs and other forage to opportunistically feeding trout.

*Baetis* can hatch throughout the season, but the heaviest and most predictable hatches occur in the spring and fall. When there have been *Baetis* hatches, a drowned *Baetis* spinner included in a Hopper-Copper-Dropper or nymph rig can be very effective. *Baetis* hatches can be prolific and the drowned spinners are a familiar and readily accepted meal, and no doubt many are consumed throughout the season. Just like the bodies of the adults, the spinners have an array of colors ranging from white to dark brown but most of them are rust or

**Facing:** When the sun is getting low it is a magical and surreal time of the day, made even better when casting to a pod of fish eating Rusty Spinners. With the low light it is very difficult to see a single spinner fished in the surface film, but a size 16 rust-bodied Vis-A-Dun with a white wing is easily seen. A VAD–Drowned Spinner combo will make fishing a low-light spinner fall pretty easy. LANDON MAYER PHOTO

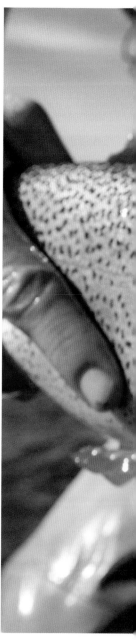

It is a real adrenalin pumper to see the riseform of a fish of this size eating Trico spinners.
JAY NICHOLS PHOTO

This nice cutthroat took a sunken spinner on the Dream Stream. When there are no aquatic insect hatches or mayfly spinner falls, trout feed opportunistically on whatever the current brings them, and throughout the season this includes drowned spinners. Trout do not eat all of the spinners during the actual spinner fall, and the uneaten spinners become waterlogged and sink, and water hydraulics also sink many spinners. They are carried downstream, and many are eaten by trout throughout the day. JAY NICHOLS PHOTO

# Drowned Trico Spinner

- **Hook:** #18-22 Lightning Strike SE5
- **Thread:** Black 8/0 UNI-Thread
- **Tail:** Pale dun hackle fibers
- **Body:** Black 8/0 UNI-Thread
- **Wings:** White Antron
- **Thorax:** Black Super Fine dubbing

olive, and I have found that a rusty pattern in sizes 18 to 22 is all that is needed. Patterns representing drowned *Baetis* spinners should be in every nymph box. I have read that some *Baetis* species can produce traditional spinner falls, but in the waters I fish I have never seen one.

Tricos can hatch almost every day on some rivers starting in July and continuing into the fall. Tricos do produce a spinner fall, sometimes in massive numbers, and they are consumed by trout throughout the summer and fall. Trico spinners are eaten from the surface during the spinner fall, but the uneaten spinners end up drowned and many are consumed subsurface throughout the day after the spinner fall has finished. During Trico season a drowned Trico spinner pattern is always a good choice when setting up a nymph or HCD rig.

Throughout the year trout see more *Baetis* and Trico drowned spinners than those of all the other mayfly species combined, but seasonally spinners of other species are important and should be carried. The widespread PMDs and many other mayfly species have rust or olive spinners, but I only carry the rust color. For whatever reason, trout love Rusty Spinners, and I carry Drowned Rusty Spinners in sizes 14 to 18 to match the naturals. If PMDs have been hatching, even if you have not been on the water during the spinner fall, a Drowned Rusty Spinner can be an effective pattern in a nymph or HCD rig.

Some mayflies, most notably the Western and Eastern Green Drakes, create spinner falls but they usually occur just before dark and during the night or very early in the morning. Fish feed on them, but it is

difficult to fish for them when the lighting is poor or nonexistent. The good news is trout will take a drowned spinner pattern throughout the day when there has been Green Drake activity. An interesting fact is even though both of the mayflies are called Green Drakes, they are not closely related and are in different families. Western Green Drakes produce rust and olive spinners, but all that is needed is a size 10 or 12 Drowned Rusty Spinner. Eastern Green Drakes produce a cream to white spinner, and a matching drowned spinner in size 8 or 10 is a good choice for a nymph or HCD rig.

You do not need to time a spinner fall when using a drowned spinner as a nymph. Trout can become ultra-selective when feeding on a spinner fall, but they are usually opportunistic when feeding subsurface. Though the fish may react more positively to a particular insect that is prominent in the drift, such as nymphs just before a hatch or drowned spinners from a recent spinner fall, most often trout feed opportunistically and will eat most drifting subsurface food that they see. Drowned spinners are a familiar sight and readily accepted throughout the day along with the other nymphs and larvae that randomly drift by.

Don't wait until you see the first spinner fall and tell yourself you need to stock up on spinners. Once mayflies start hatching, which is usually early spring, drowned spinner patterns are always a good option. I use the same drowned patterns when nymph fishing or as a dropper when fishing a spinner fall for rising fish.

I use the same setup when fishing a spinner fall as I do when fishing a hatch. I like a fast-action 9-foot 3-weight rod, a 3-weight

The droppers I most often use when fishing an HCD rig or for rising trout. Sunken spinners occupy an important row.
JAKE BURLESON PHOTO

Fishing a spinner fall on the Colorado River. Spinners are dead and do not move, and it is essential that your flies reach the fish totally drag-free. JAY NICHOLS PHOTO

WF floating line with a dry-fly taper, and a 9-foot 5X leader. I add around 24 inches of 6X fluorocarbon to the leader using a five-turn blood knot and attach a Vis-A-Dun with a body that is the same size and color as the natural spinner to the 6X with a five-turn clinch knot. I tie around 8 inches of 6X fluorocarbon to the bend of the Vis-A-Dun with a five-turn clinch knot and tie on the drowned spinner with the same knot. I usually use 6X, but sometimes conditions may call for 7X.

When fishing a nymph or HCD rig, I use a fast-action 9-foot 4-weight rod and a 4-weight WF floating line with the taper more heavily weighted towards the front of the head to aid in casting and turning over the nymph or HCD rig. I use a 7½-foot 2X leader and add fluorocarbon tippet starting with 3X. I will add 4X to 6X fluorocarbon tippet depending on what flies I am using and the conditions. I usually use 4X for the large spinners and 5X or 6X for the smaller spinners.

**Facing:** The Trico fish netted and displayed by Landon Mayer. The spinner fall was heavy and a single Trico spinner pattern fished in the surface film would disappear among the naturals, but the white-winged Vis-A-Dun was very visible and when the trout took the drowned spinner the VAD disappeared. JAY NICHOLS PHOTO

# PLAYING FISH

To properly play a fish and land it in a timely manner you must smoothly control the rod, reel, and line and coordinate these actions with what the fish is doing. Some people are ambidextrous and can use both hands with equal skill, but most of us have a dominant hand. Fly fishers should cast, mend line, and fight fish while holding the rod in their dominant hand and reel and strip in line with the other hand.

Before I start fishing I set the drag fairly light, just heavy enough so that when I rip out line or when a fish goes on a high-speed run it won't backlash. I get a real thrill when a fish goes on a run, which is a big reason why I set my drag light.

How you fight a fish largely depends on the size and strength of the fish. Small fish are easy to play and land because you can basically strip them in, but when you hook a larger fish more skill is required. After a large fish is hooked, make sure there is no loose line wrapped around anything and do not try to stop him. Do nothing except hold the grip and just let the fish run or power thrash. When the fish has settled down, you can start fighting him.

During the initial run the only drag applied on the fish is what the reel supplies. Since the drag setting on my reel is light, I have to be able to increase the drag over that which the reel supplies while I am fighting the fish. I control the

Fighting a quality fish that was fooled by a drowned Trico spinner fished under a black-bodied Vis-A-Dun, using 6X fluorocarbon tippet to both flies, while fishing a Trico spinner fall on the Dream Stream in Colorado. JAY NICHOLS PHOTO

137

## PLAYING FISH

To obtain the best control I like to maintain a low rod position when a fish is running. I raise the tip only if a fish is running towards structure. Hopefully the fish swims around the structure, and I want my leader and tippet to clear it. While a fish is running the only drag applied is with the reel.

When the fish has stopped running, I like to pinch the line against the grip with the middle finger of my right hand while keeping a grip on the reel handle with my left hand. I pump the fish towards me while keeping maximum pressure, and I keep the line pinched against the grip while reeling in line. When line is being reeled in, I loosen the pinch of my right middle finger against the grip and tighten it again as I lower the rod tip towards the fish to resume pumping and reeling.

If the fish takes off, I let go of the line and let the fish run and let the reel's drag continue pressure on the fish.

When the fish has been brought into netting position and tired out, I lock him down, being ready to instantly let go of the line if he takes off. Once subdued, the fish can be netted.

drag pressure by pinching the line against the rod grip with my fore and middle finger and varying the amount of pressure from a light pinch to a max lockdown depending on what the fish is doing.

While fighting a fish it is important to keep constant and maximum pressure and never let him rest. If the fish isn't running, you should be gaining line. When the fish is trying to rest, use maximum pressure to pinch the line against the grip and pull the fish towards you. As you pull the fish towards you, reel in line. If the fish wants to run, let go of the line and let him run. When the fish rests, lock him down and pump and reel until you land him.

The lower you keep the rod during the fight, the greater control you have over the fish and the more pressure you can apply with the rod. You apply very little pressure on the fish when your rod tip is pointing up, and it is difficult to control the fish when the rod tip is more vertical. You may need to raise the rod up to stay tight to the fish or to keep the line and leader clear of obstructions while a fish is running, but try to try keep it as low as possible during the fight.

Many fly fishers do not realize how much pressure they can put on light tippet material. Andy Mills, one of the most accomplished anglers of our time, landed a 70-pound tarpon on 4X. That gives you a pretty good idea of the capabilities of modern-day light tippet material. To see how much pressure you can put on various tippets, rig up a 5-weight rod with a 2X leader and add a 3X tippet, tie on a fly, and stick it into a tree at ground level and pretend you are fighting a fish. Keep increasing the pressure until you break the tippet. Repeat the exercise with 4X, 5X, and 6X tippet. With a proper bend in the rod and a smooth, steady pull, you will be amazed how much pressure you can exert before you break the tippet.

I remember talking to someone who was holding a saltwater seminar and had a 12-weight rod rigged up. He tied the line to a scale and asked people to really lean on the rod. Very few of the people registered over 5 pounds of pressure on the scale, which wouldn't break 4X. You can imagine how little pressure most people apply with a light trout rod.

The point is, don't worry about the breaking strength of the tippet as long as you have a proper bend in the rod and you are applying smooth, steady pressure. Tippets most often fail because of poorly tied knots or tippet abrasion, or when sudden jerks are transmitted to the leader when setting the fly too hard or when clamping down on the fly line or reel handle when a fish is running or thrashing.

An important variable determining how much pressure to exert when fighting a fish is the size of the fly. When putting pressure on a fish, a smaller fly is more likely to pull out than a larger fly because it has less of a purchase in the fish's flesh. You can still put solid pressure on the fish, and it is surprising how much force can be exerted on a big fish if the small fly is embedded solidly in the fish's jaw.

I remember hooking a large-bodied 20-inch brown on a size 22 Trico spinner with a 6X tippet. I fought the fish hard until it went to the bottom of a pool and Velcroed himself to the sand. I could see the fish, the leader was not hung up on anything, but he just would not swim. I decided to apply smooth, heavy pressure to the fish, knowing that either the fly would get ripped out or I would move him. I put the rod tip in the water and with a smooth motion raised the rod up so only the bottom half of my 3-weight rod was bent and the top half was almost straight. He relented his position and I landed him. I was amazed at how much pressure I put on that fish with 6X and a size 22 fly, and that everything held.

Many things can compromise a released fish's health, but I feel the greatest damage is from overplaying them. A hooked and struggling fish is being oxygen deprived and is building up damaging metabolic toxins. The longer a fish is fought, the greater the negative effect on the fish's health. While playing fish I see some fly fishers putting a fraction of the pressure on fish that they could. Sometimes I see people just holding the rod grip, applying very little pressure, and allowing the fish to swim around until it is almost dead before they land it. If it doesn't die from the high level of toxins built up and the oxygen deprivation to its tissues, especially the brain, it is so stressed out that it will take a long time to recover and resume feeding. Luckily if the oxygen deprivation and toxic buildup do not exceed a critical level, the effects are reversible and after a little time to recover the fish will be fine. Many people play fish gingerly and tentatively because they don't want to lose them. They should do the exact opposite and be aggressive and apply maximum pressure throughout the fight, never letting the fish rest.

The longer you play a fish, the greater the odds are that you will lose it. The longer the fight lasts, the greater the odds are that your leader can weaken from tooth abrasion or from rubbing or hanging up on underwater structure. The longer a fish is in the water, the greater the likelihood that it may find something to wrap the leader around and break off. During a prolonged battle the fly can loosen and come out when a fish thrashes or jumps, and you increase the odds of pilot error such as getting your fly line wrapped around any of many threats such as loose clothing, fingers, reel handles, or rod butts. I cannot overemphasize how important it is for the fish's well-being to land them as quickly as possible.

## 6

# LAKE RISERS

I enjoy blind-fishing, but when I find rising fish during a hatch in either rivers or lakes, the level of excitement and anticipation instantly amps up. The tactics for fishing hatches in stillwaters are quite different from those used in rivers. When trout are rising in rivers they usually stay in one small area and wait for the current to bring them the hatching insects, and it is not that difficult to get positioned and make an accurate delivery. It may not be easy to get a take, but at least you know the trout will see your fly. Stillwaters don't have current and the fish must constantly swim while searching for the hatching insects, and after they feed they keep swimming.

When the sun starts to set and the light on the water is diminishing, big trout will often leave the deeper water and cruise near shore. This area is forage rich and with the reduced light the big fish feel more comfortable feeding in the shallow water. JAY NICHOLS PHOTO

The most difficult challenge when casting to rising trout in lakes is where to cast after a fish feeds so that the fish will see your fly. The quicker you deliver your fly after a fish rises, the better the chances are that the fish will see and hopefully take it. When a fish eats with a head and tail rise, especially if it rises more than once, you have a pretty good idea which direction it is going. The fish is still swimming, so the fly needs to be delivered quickly, but at least you have a clue of the direction of travel. If a fish boils it is impossible to determine which direction it is swimming after it feeds, and the quicker you get your fly near the riseform,

the greater the odds that the fish will see it. Every second counts, and the longer it takes to complete the cast, the greater the odds that the fish is no longer close to where it rose. A bit of good news is a fish that feeds on or just under the surface will sometimes hesitate or momentarily slow down as it eats the insect.

Fishing to surface-feeding trout in lakes is always a challenge, but after years of trial and error I have developed a method I call the rapid delivery technique that not only works well but is a lot of fun. This technique is used most effectively when fishing from a float tube, but some of the principles of the

The *Callibaetis* mayfly is the most important stillwater mayfly for fly fishers. It is widespread and has multiple broods, providing opportunities for fly fishers throughout the season. Fish rising during a *Callibaetis* hatch can be effectively fished with a double nymph or double dry combo. Both rigs are effective, but the higher percentage setup is a double nymph rig because the cruising trout usually don't follow a predictable path and there is a better chance a trout will see one of your nymphs as you are retrieving them rather than the stationary floating dry flies. JAY NICHOLS PHOTO

Fishing to a *Callibaetis* gulper on Antero Reservoir in Colorado. JAY NICHOLS PHOTO

technique can also be applied when wade fishing, fishing from shore to fish feeding in deeper water, or fishing from a boat.

The key component of the technique is having line stripped out and trailing in the water while you are looking for rises. While you slowly kick backward in a float tube the line, leader, and flies will be trailing in the water in front of you. You want to keep the rod and line in a straight line to keep slack out of the line so that it instantly responds when you raise the rod to begin the cast. If you are wading, hold the rod so it is pointing behind you with the line trailing.

Whether in a float tube or wading, I like to have enough line trailing in the water so that the rear of the head is just sticking out of the tip-top guide. In addition I like to keep some running line stripped out so I can shoot it in case a longer cast is needed. If a fish rises closer than the amount of line and leader that is trailing, I make some rapid strips of the line before starting the cast and if needed I will elevate the rod tip when delivering the fly, which will further shorten the cast.

When fishing from a float tube, if I see a rise I pick the line off of the water, make a

# STILLWATER RIGGING

I use the same rod, line, and leader setup when fishing hatches on lakes as I do when indicator fishing with nymphs in both rivers and lakes. I like a 9-foot fast-action 4-weight rod and a WF floating line with most of the weight concentrated in the forward part of the head. The line taper is very important. I use a 7½-foot 2X leader and add fluorocarbon tippet. The fast-action rod picks up the line quickly, and aided by the line's taper the flies can be delivered rapidly. Remember, the sooner your fly arrives after you see a rise, the better the odds of hooking the fish.

When deciding what size tippet to use, I consider several factors including weather, water conditions, and the size of the fish. If it is sunny with no wind and the water is clear, I will usually use lighter tippets than if the water is off-color and it is breezy and overcast. In addition to water and weather conditions, the size of the fish is a big factor when choosing the tippet. If there is a good chance of hooking a real heavyweight, no matter the conditions I use heavier tippet even though it might result in some refusals.

I always use fluorocarbon. The first tippet section is around 20 inches and always 3X. I usually attach the first fly to the 3X, but if I am going to use 4X to the first fly, I make the 3X section around 10 inches and attach about 20 inches of 4X.

Big *Callibaetis* fish going deep into the backing. LANDON MAYER PHOTO

Big thrash as the *Callibaetis*-eating fish is almost ready to net. LANDON MAYER PHOTO

I tie around 24 inches of either 3X or 4X to the hook bend of the first fly and tie on the second fly. Having a good separation between the first and second fly increases the odds of a fish seeing one of the flies. Even though I sometimes use 5X, I like to avoid it because some takes are unexpected and because the fish are swimming it is easy to break fish off. Usually in stillwaters you can get by using heavier tippets than you can when fishing a hatch in rivers.

I use a five-turn blood knot to attach the 3X tippet to the 2X leader and to knot the 4X tippet to the 3X. I use a five-turn clinch knot to attach the flies and the leader to the hook bend of the first fly.

backcast, and ideally deliver the fly on the first forward cast. If the fish is not in front of me, a second or third false cast may be necessary to get the fly tracking in the right direction. If I see a rise while wade fishing, I pick the line off the water with a forward cast, and ideally make one backcast and deliver the fly. It is very important with this rapid delivery technique to develop line speed quickly, so I double-haul both the back and forward casts. Another positive about fishing the rapid delivery system is that with the flies trailing in the water as you look for rises, you will hook fish on the troll.

There are three groups of aquatic insects that hatch in stillwaters that produce the most opportunities for fly fishers: midges, mayflies, and damselflies. I fish the same rapid delivery technique for all three groups of insects.

## Midges

The many species of stillwater midges all have the same life cycle. After hatching the adult midges mate and the female flies low over the water and taps her abdomen on the surface and releases her fertilized eggs, which sink to the bottom. The eggs hatch into larvae just like caddis and live and feed in the bottom substrate and keep growing until mature, then they stop feeding. They create a silken covering, and inside this protective covering they transform into pupae.

Inside the pupal sheath an amazing transformation from the pupa into the adult midge takes place and when ready, the adult still inside the pupal shuck swims to the surface. At this stage it is considered a pupa but technically it is an adult inside a shuck that looks like a pupa. After reaching the surface the adult wriggles around until the shuck splits open and it hatches.

Depending on conditions, the adults can float on the surface for a while after hatching, but usually they soon start buzzing around while drying their wings or sometimes they take off shortly after hatching. Some adults are eaten during a midge hatch, but the pupae are the easiest target for trout. Most feeding during a midge hatch is on the pupae, and a pupa pattern is usually the most effective fly to use.

You can get a pretty good idea what size pupa to use by looking at the hatching adult. I always fish two pupa patterns, with the trailing fly one size smaller than the first fly, because I am never sure exactly what size to use and often there are multiple species hatching that are different sizes. A nice thing about fishing a midge hatch is you can usually get by with fishing a larger pupa pattern than the pupae that are hatching.

Most pupae are either a black-and-white zebra pattern or red, and those are the two colors I carry in a variety of sizes. A significant development that noticeably increased the number of takes was when I started tying my midge pupa patterns with a black flashback wing case. I think the biggest reason was it helped fish find the flies in addition to the fish-attracting qualities of a little subtle flash.

After delivering the flies to a rise, make sure your rod and line are in a straight line before starting your retrieve, which will ensure direct contact with your fly. After making a cast, I like to make a quick strip of 8 to 12 inches to get the fish's attention, then continue the retrieve using hand twists

# Electric Midge Pupa

- **Hook:** #10-16 Lightning Strike SE5
- **Thread:** Black 140-denier UTC Ultra Thread
- **Body:** Black 140-denier UTC Ultra Thread
- **Rib:** Blue-silver flake Holographic Flashabou and silver UTC Ultra Wire (brassie)
- **Body coating:** UV-cured resin
- **Thorax:** Black Super Fine dubbing
- **Gills:** White Antron
- **Wing case:** Black Flashback Tinsel (large)
- **Note:** This all-around midge pupa can also be an effective trailer behind a streamer when fishing a streamer-trailer combo.

Hiking into a bay on Spinney Mountain Reservoir, Colorado. LANDON MAYER PHOTO

of various speeds with pauses throughout. During the pause the pupa will sink, and when the retrieve is resumed the floating line will lift the pupa and look to the fish like a pupa swimming to the surface. I suggest using a variety of retrieves and see what is the most effective. When a fish takes the fly I just stay tight, and since the fish is swimming it will usually set the hook.

## Mayflies

Only a few species of mayflies hatch in coldwater lakes, and probably the most important to the trout fisher are species in the *Callibaetis* genus and to a lesser extent species in the *Tricorythodes* genus. Perhaps the most famous lake hatch to the general populace is the *Hexagenia* hatch in the Great Lakes, where billions of the monster mayflies hatch every year and videos of them are shown on newscasts across the country, covering everything on the ground and sometimes showing up on radar. I could find nothing on the internet about fishing the Hex hatch in lakes, only in rivers.

Species in the *Callibaetis* genus are the most important mayfly for fly fishers because they are widespread and have multiple broods throughout the season. I have read about Trico hatches and spinner falls that occur in Hebgen Lake in Montana and provide a great opportunity for the fly fisher, but I have never fished a Trico hatch

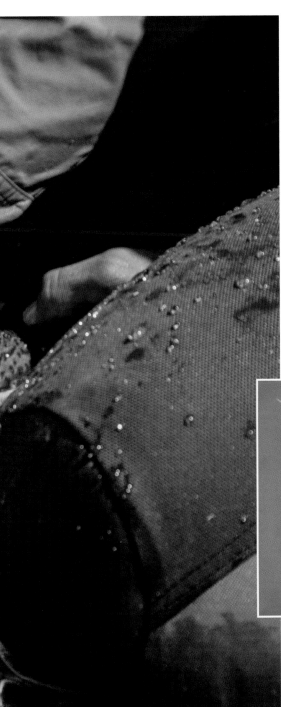

or spinner fall in lakes. The Trico hatches I have seen are unpredictable and occurred at the same time that *Callibaetis* were hatching so maybe fish were taking both insects, but Calli patterns always worked so I never bothered fishing Trico patterns. I will have to defer to Hebgen Lake experts on how to fish lake Tricos.

Stillwater mayflies have the same life cycle as mayflies in rivers and streams, but my approach to fishing them is different. Depending on conditions, how long they sit on the surface varies, but usually it takes a while for the wings to dry. At this time adult mayflies are easier targets than adult midges, and an adult pattern can be productive. During a hatch stillwater trout are cruising, sometimes fairly fast, in search of the hatching insects and don't scrutinize their prey as carefully as trout feeding

*Callibaetis* spinner. LANDON MAYER PHOTO

*Callibaetis* nymphs come in many colors, from ginger to tan to olive, and in Antero that day many of the nymphs were olive. A green Copper John was readily accepted by this rainbow. JAY NICHOLS PHOTO

153

Landon Mayer getting ready to land a nice rainbow that had been feeding during a *Callibaetis* hatch on Antero Reservoir near Fairplay, Colorado. JAY NICHOLS PHOTO

during a hatch in rivers. One should use good imitations, but pattern selection is not as critical as when fishing a hatch in a river.

In describing how I fish a stillwater mayfly hatch, I am going to specifically reference the *Callibaetis* group of mayflies because that is the mayfly hatch I have most often fished. There are not that many species of stillwater mayflies, and the technique I use when fishing a Calli hatch will work for any of them.

During a *Callibaetis* hatch fish feed on the nymphs, emergers, and adults but primarily the nymphs and adults because the dun usually escapes the exoskeleton (shuck) rapidly and the emergent stage is not as available to the trout as the nymph and dun. When fishing a Calli hatch with the rapid delivery system, the only option is to fish nymphs because trolling dry flies will sink them. I like to use two nymphs, which increases the odds of a fish seeing one of them. I troll the

Selecting flies for the *Callibaetis* hatch. When fishing a Calli hatch you need to come equipped with nymphs and duns. You should also carry spinners when the spinners come back to the lake to mate, lay eggs, and fall to the surface. A lot of what flies you use depends on how you feel like fishing. You will probably hook more fish using double nymphs but you don't get the thrill of a dry-fly eat. LANDON MAYER PHOTO

nymphs while slowly kicking my float tube, all the while looking for rising fish. If I see a rise that is in casting range, I quickly pick up the trolled flies and make a cast to the rising fish as fast as I can.

Because you are covering a lot of water while trolling the flies, the odds of a cruising fish seeing your flies are increased more than if you just hold your flies and wait for a rise. The fish you initially target with your nymph may not take it right away but may follow it, so you want to retrieve the fly all the way back to the rod. The fish may take it during the retrieve or another fish may take it. If not, make another cast and resuming trolling.

There are many *Callibaetis* nymph patterns, and they all work. The nymphs can vary in color from olive to ginger depending on individual color variation or the habitat they live in, but trout aren't really selective to color when feeding during a hatch. I like to fish a pure copper Copper John trailed by any of the *Callibaetis*-specific nymphs. There are a number of species of *Callibaetis* and the size can decrease as the season progresses, but a size 14 nymph trailed by a size 16 usually works well.

After I deliver the flies to a rise, I make a quick strip of 8 to 12 inches to get the fish's attention then continue the retrieve with a variety of hand twists mixed with an occasional strip. The most important thing is to deliver the flies as soon as you can after seeing a rise. During a hatch stillwater trout are cruising, sometimes fairly fast, in search of the hatching insects and don't scrutinize

A selection of damselfly and *Callibaetis* patterns. LANDON MAYER PHOTO

flies as carefully as trout feeding during a hatch in rivers. You should use good imitations, but pattern selection is not as critical as when fishing a hatch in a river.

When using the rapid delivery technique when fishing a *Callibaetis* hatch, I always use 3X fluorocarbon tippet, and even then if a fast-cruising heavyweight takes one of your flies, it can easily pop the 3X if you don't react properly. Even though 4X or 5X may get more takes, the probability of breaking off a big fish is quite high.

The odds of showing your flies to more fish when fishing nymphs with the rapid delivery system are far greater than when a dry fly is sitting in one spot, and I also feel that trout are more likely to eat a sub-surface pattern than one that is floating. If you want to fish dry flies, however, I recommend using two flies, but you will have to remain stationary and cast the flies and let them sit on the surface until you see a fish rise. Then you can pick up, make a false cast to dry the flies, and deliver them to where you think the fish is heading. Fish that are cruising that have not risen can also take one of your flies while it is sitting.

When fishing a spinner fall trolling is not an option, so like when fishing dun patterns you can't move around much and have to wait for the fish to come to you. Your only option is to fish two floating spinner patterns totally motionless, since the natural spinner patterns you are imitating are dead and motionless. I like a hackled pattern such as a gray Vis-A-Dun for my first fly and a spent floating pattern for my second. I don't use drowned spinners in lakes because there are no currents in lakes like in rivers where natural spinners become drowned.

## Damselflies

Midge and mayfly nymphs hatch in the water, but damselfly nymphs crawl out of the water and hatch on land, just like stoneflies. Damselflies have three stages in their life cycle—egg, nymph, and adult—just like mayflies and stoneflies. When damselfly nymphs are mature, they migrate from their home in the aquatic weed beds to shore. These migrations can contain huge numbers of nymphs, which creates a feeding frenzy with the trout and in turn an incredible opportunity for the fly fisher.

Damselflies and dragonflies have been around for over 300 million years, and other than getting smaller they have remained anatomically almost unchanged during that time. It has been said by some scientists that they are nature's most perfect design, and their life cycle is pretty impressive for an insect. It starts with a fertilized egg that a female has deposited in an aquatic weed bed, plant stem, or rotting wood. The fertilized eggs hatch into nymphs, and they almost immediately start feeding and growing. Damselfly nymphs have the same protective exoskeleton that mayfly and stonefly nymphs have, and it is shed and regenerated as the nymphs feed and grow. When mature the nymphs quit feeding and like mayflies and stoneflies make the miraculous transformation to adults while still in the final protective exoskeleton.

When ready to hatch the nymphs leave the protection of the weed beds where they had been living and begin swimming towards the shore. The nymphs, technically adults still inside the nymphal shuck, crawl out of the water and just like stoneflies crawl

Most stillwaters contain damselflies, and although they usually don't have multiple broods, the nymphs don't all mature at the same time so the hatch can extend for many weeks. When the mature nymphs are swimming to shore to hatch, trout cruise the perimeter of the lake picking off as many nymphs as they can. This nice rainbow saw the slowly stripped damselfly nymph imitation and crushed it. JAY NICHOLS PHOTO

onto various structure such as a stick, rock, or cattail, where they wriggle around until the nymphal shuck splits and they hatch into a pale green young adult. They cling to where they hatched while their wings dry, and when ready they fly away. Males take on a blue color and most females a tan color, although some are blue like the males.

The adults become sexually mature quickly, and some start mating days after hatching. Mating takes place on land, and while mating the male grasps the female behind her head with claspers on the tip of his abdomen. They join together and the sperm is transferred to the female. We have all seen damselflies perched on various structure such as sticks, grass blades, or rocks while they are mating. While joined their bodies create a heart-shaped silhouette referred to as the wheel position.

After fertilization the female is ready to lay her eggs. During egg laying an interesting phenomenon occurs that is unique to both damselflies and dragonflies. The male and female often fly in tandem, with the male flying lead and grasping the female behind her head with his claspers. This behavior is to protect the female from other males, and they usually stay coupled while she lays her eggs.

The female lays her eggs in floating weed mats, or while still joined the male and female may swim underwater and crawl down sticks or aquatic weeds, and she lays her eggs in aquatic plant stems, mats of submerged algae, or rotting wood. The female has a structure on or near the tip of her abdomen that is sharp, and she uses it to make a little slice into where she chooses to deposit her eggs and then releases the eggs into this opening. She usually repeats this egg-laying process in more than one location.

Damselflies can stay submerged for up to thirty minutes, so they can take their time finding ideal spots. After egg laying is completed, damselflies don't die like mayflies but rather swim to the surface and fly away. They are able to eat and are voracious predators, consuming midges, mosquitoes, and any other insect they can capture. They can live for weeks, some even months, during which time they will mate several times and lay many more eggs and the cycle will repeat itself.

During a damselfly hatch assume that almost all of the fish are feeding on the nymphs and not the occasional adult that flies over the water. The nymphs are much more numerous and easier for a fish to eat than a flying adult. The nymphs swim slowly and sometimes for quite a distance before reaching shore, making them very vulnerable to predation by the trout. You may see some adults flying above the surface and some trout trying to nail them, but their success rate is quite low and even though trout can be caught on an adult pattern, it is a low-percentage approach.

Unlike the clumsy, weak-flying stoneflies that are doomed if they get in the water, damsels are strong fliers and even if an adult inadvertently gets blown into the water by a wind gust, it won't become trapped by the surface film and will quickly fly away. The easiest target for the trout is the nymph, and most trout are looking for and feeding on the nymphs. Anything is possible in nature and I know people catch trout on adult damsels, but maybe that same trout would have taken a hopper or any other dry fly. The only time adult damselflies spend much time over the water is just prior to egg laying, which usually takes place in weed beds and other areas that generally are not very accessible to trout, and not that many adults are eaten by trout.

Although most adult females are tan and all males are blue, there is no color difference between male and female nymphs. The color of the nymphs can range from tan to olive depending on individual variation and where they live, and trout feed opportunistically on all of the colors during a hatch. I just tie one damselfly nymph using a mixture of tan and olive dubbing. There are many good damselfly nymph patterns, and whatever fly or color damselfly nymph you choose to use will work just fine. I always fish two flies, a size 10 trailed by a size 12. There are not that

# Barr's Damselfly Nymph

- **Hook:** #10-14 TMC 5262
- **Thread:** Olive 80-denier UTC Ultra Thread
- **Tail:** Olive marabou
- **Body:** Watery olive and tan Sow Scud dubbing, mixed 50/50
- **Over body:** Olive/black Fly Specks Thin Skin
- **Rib:** Fluorocarbon
- **Thorax:** Same dubbing mix as body
- **Legs:** Olive Hungarian partridge
- **Eyes:** 60-pound mono, burned
- **Thorax:** Same dubbing mix as body

Nice damsel-eating brown on Antero Reservoir caught while fishing with Landon Mayer from his new Hog Island skiff.
LANDON MAYER PHOTO

Damselfly eater taking off. Damselflies can hatch at the same time of year as *Callibaetis*, so patterns representing both insects should be in your box when fishing a lake during hatch time. The nymphs swim to shore, where they crawl out of the water onto reeds, sticks, and other available structure and hatch. Trout feast on the nymphs as they slowly swim to shore, and once they hatch the adults are rarely seen by trout. LANDON MAYER PHOTO

many species of stillwater damselflies, and these two sizes will match the size of most of the nymphs.

The rapid delivery system is a very effective technique when fishing a damselfly hatch. Plenty of trout are hooked on the troll, and when you see a rise quickly pick your line off the water and make a rapid delivery to where you hope the fish is. I make an 8- to 12-inch strip after the flies hit the water and continue the retrieve using a variety of hand twists and strips, just like I use when fishing midge pupas and *Callibaetis* nymphs. Sometimes a fish will follow your fly, so fish it all the way in and resume trolling if you don't get a hookup. I always use 3X fluorocarbon tippet when fishing a damselfly hatch because some of the lake's superheavyweights often come to feed during a damselfly migration.

# STREAMERS

Most fly fishers fish streamers the same way. They use the time-honored techniques using sink-tip or full-sinking lines and a relatively short leader. In a river the angler lets the current swing the streamer through likely holding water, while imparting a variety of strips. In a lake the streamer is cast and allowed to sink, then the fly is retrieved. The fly is always on a tight line so the angler instantly feels when a fish takes the fly and the hook is set. This is an effective way to fish, and I have done it this way for years.

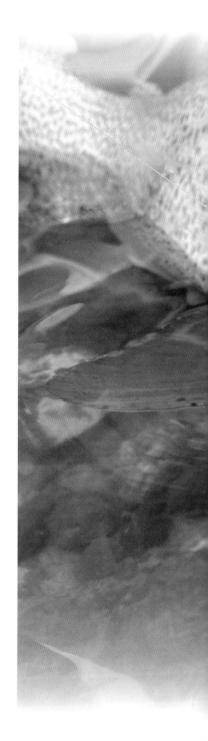

Heavyweight caught by Landon Mayer in Colorado's Dream Stream that crushed a black Hot Cone Slumpbuster. It is a killer pattern for high and/or off-colored water and an excellent choice during spawning season when the testosterone is flowing and the males become aggressive and territorial. LANDON MAYER PHOTO

However, over the years I have developed another method that I call the passive streamer technique, which doesn't replace the time-honored retrieve above but rather adds another dimension. Basically the technique employs a floating line, a longer leader than what is used with a sinking line, and a streamer tied on a jig hook with a brass or tungsten cone, which causes the fly to ride hook point up. The fly is fished very slowly with lots of pauses during the retrieve, and takes are usually subtle versus the slam felt when stripping streamers on a tight line. Many of the fish take the fly as it is sinking after a cast or when it is dropping while pausing during the retrieve. Takes are detected by watching the line for unnatural movement like old-style nymphing, or feeling for little taps or ticks on the line during the retrieve.

All predators including mammals, birds, and fish eat healthy prey, but they are always on the lookout for the ones that are weak, injured, or dying. Disabled prey is easier and requires less energy to capture, and if a predator sees disabled prey mixed in with fast and elusive healthy individuals, it will opt for the easier target. Wolf packs search for elk and deer that are weakened because of injury or starvation. Birds of prey look for dead or wounded animals, and predatory fish are always on the lookout for

Tying on a Virile Meat Whistle with a five-turn clinch knot. Ginger and blue is a deadly streamer color combination.
JAKE BURLESON PHOTO

A cruising smallmouth was spotted, and after a quick strip followed by a slow hand-twist retrieve the fish crushed a Meat Whistle.

prey that is injured or otherwise vulnerable. Predacious fish will pursue any prey they think they can capture, but if there is a slow-moving, struggling target, they will take the easy meal over one that is more difficult to catch. We have all had large fish try to eat a small fish that we have hooked that is struggling and unable to flee while we play it. Predator fish are always on the lookout for the easiest target, and this is the principle on which the passive streamer technique is based.

For many years when fishing subsurface for largemouth and smallmouth bass, I often used conventional gear. I still fly fished, but the conventional setup was more productive and allowed me to fish water that I couldn't effectively fish with a fly, plus I really enjoyed it. My favorite subsurface bait was a skirted jig with a twin-tailed trailer. It creates an excellent illusion of a crawdad, which is an important food source for bass and trout, and just suggests something good to eat, and it is lethal. The slow manner in which it is fished suggests prey that may be injured and vulnerable, which is a trigger for predatory fish.

I enjoyed fishing conventional gear and it was deadly, but my real passion was fly fishing and I decided it was time to try to come up with a fly that looked and fished like a jig and trailer and was as effective. I also needed to develop a technique that would allow me to fish a fly setup in the same manner that I fished a jig and trailer with conventional gear.

When designing the fly I used a skirted lead-headed jig with a twin-tailed plastic trailer as the template. When retrieved, the jig and trailer comes through the water with the hook point riding up, and it can be fished on the bottom and through weeds with minimal hang-ups. I wanted the fly to have these same attributes, so for starters it had to be tied on a jig hook.

I knew nothing about jig hooks, but luckily my friend Cliff Watts had spent many years and lots of trial and error finding the best jig hook for his deadly steelhead

This smallmouth inhaled a Virile Meat Whistle passively fished on the bottom.

# Hot Cone Slumpbuster

- **Hook:** #2-6 TMC 5263
- **Thread:** 140-denier UTC Ultra Thread
- **Cone:** Fluorescent orange brass or tungsten (large)
- **Tail:** Black pine squirrel
- **Body:** Royal blue Sparkle Braid with black pine squirrel pulled over the top and ribbed with blue UTC Ultra Wire (brassie)
- **Flash:** Royal blue Holographic Flashabou
- **Collar:** Black pine squirrel
- **Note:** I first tied this fly for a friend of mine who was going to Kamchatka in pursuit of the monster rainbows because I thought it might be a good pattern. When he returned he said it was the hottest pattern the week he was there and he ended the trip as the top rod, with the most and the biggest fish of the week, all caught on a Hot Cone Slumpbuster. The fly is also a very productive pattern for Alaska rainbows as well as big trout in the Lower 48.

# Meat Whistle (Virile)

- **Hook:** #3/0-1 Gamakatsu Jig 90
- **Thread:** Wood duck 140-denier UTC Ultra Thread
- **Cone:** Gold tungsten (large)
- **Tail:** Ginger rabbit strip
- **Body:** Royal blue Sparkle Braid
- **Over body:** Ginger rabbit strip
- **Rib:** Blue UTC Ultra Wire (brassie)
- **Collar:** Ginger marabou and blue-silver flake Sili Legs
- **Flash:** Blue-silver flake Holographic Flashabou

Shortly after releasing the smallmouth I caught an actual virile crawdad, which is the common name for the most numerous species of crawdad in both flowing and still waters in Colorado. The crawdad had a firm grip on the rabbit strip tail of my fly.

pattern, the Kilowatt. Cliff is a highly respected angler and has caught hundreds of steelhead, including some monsters on the Kilowatt, which is tied on a 90-degree jig hook with bead-chain eyes. He felt the hook he used on his pattern had the best combination of hooking ability and strength of all the jig hooks he had experimented with, and I decided that was the hook I was going to use for my fly. Thank you, Cliff, for shortening the learning curve.

I started the design process by placing a tungsten or brass cone at the front of the hook. I reasoned that the cone would give the fly a nice falling and jigging action and hopefully cause the fly to ride hook point up. I tried different materials and designs.

The first prototype I liked was dressed with a rabbit strip tail, a Diamond Braid body, and a marabou collar and included flash and Sili Legs. It looked a lot like a jig and trailer. I love rabbit and marabou because the way they move and undulate in the water suggests life, and a little flash and some Sili Legs further adds to the illusion of something alive.

Before I fished the fly I tested it in a 100-gallon aquarium. I attached a length of 0X tippet to the tip section of a fly rod, tied on the fly, and tossed it into the water and observed it through the glass. It looked good and had a nice, steady sink rate. My biggest concern was that it would lie over on its side when it reached the bottom, but

## THE PASSIVE RETRIEVE

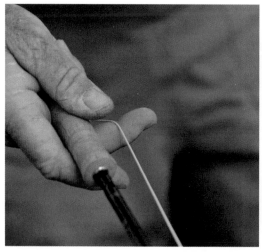

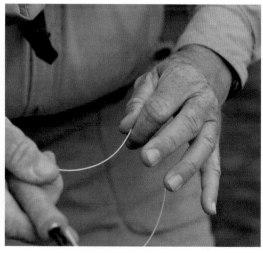

**1.** I begin the passive retrieve by draping the line over the first crease of the middle finger on my right hand, which is holding the rod grip. I will execute the retrieve with my left hand, which is behind my right hand and just to the left of the reel.

**2.** To start the hand twist, I pinch the line between the forefinger and thumb of my left hand.

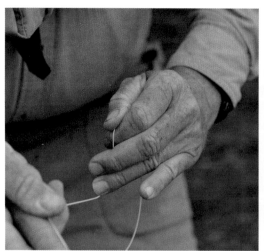

**3.** While pinching the line I retrieve the line with the last two or three fingers of my left hand while simultaneously rotating the wrist clockwise.

**4.** Beginning the hand twist.

**5.** Completing the hand twist by rotating the wrist clockwise while gripping the line between the fingers and palm of my left hand. As I am retrieving, the line stays draped over the middle finger of my right hand. While retrieving I let the line drop into a stripping basket or the water. I repeat the sequence until a fish is hooked or a fly is retrieved and ready for another cast. By continually having contact with the line, I can strip-set instantly with my left hand when a fish takes the fly.

**6.** I rotate my left wrist counterclockwise and am ready for another hand twist. The hand twist can be any speed or can be slow followed by a quick twist or two. Always include pauses during the retrieve to allow the fly to drop, which all fish love. A twist of the floating line following a pause will raise the fly, which can trigger a take just like when the fly falls.

When I detect a strike I strip-set the hook with my left hand followed almost simultaneously by firmly pressing the line against the rod grip with the middle finger of the right hand.

ALL PHOTOS BY JAY NICHOLS

I was ecstatic when it landed hook point up and the hook point remained pointing up as I jigged it along the bottom. It looked a lot like a jig and trailer, except I thought it was more lifelike and looked better.

When the fly was sitting still, the front of the hook and the cone stayed on the bottom but the rest of the hook and the rabbit strip suspended at around a 45-degree angle. While the fly sat on the bottom, the rabbit strip slowly undulated in the water and the marabou fluffed out, creating appealing bulk and undulating as well. The Sili Legs and flash helped create added appeal. I named it the Meat Whistle because the name just seemed to fit. The fly looked good to me, but how it looked to the bass was what mattered.

## Passive Streamer Technique

When I first fished the Meat Whistle, I used traditional techniques to see if it worked. I cast, let the fly sink, and stripped it in. The fly worked well using a traditional streamer technique, but now I had to figure out how to fish it using the same passive technique I used with the jig and trailer, because I had no doubt the passive technique would be more effective. There is a reason when you see the bass pros on TV fishing jigs they fish the bait using a passive technique, because at the end of the day they catch more and larger fish than if they just reeled it in.

When fishing spinning or bait-casting gear, I would cast the jig and trailer and let it sink to the bottom, where I would let it sit for a few seconds. Then I would lift the rod tip, which both raised the jig off the bottom and moved it towards me, and reel in the slack as the jig was falling back to the bottom, where I would again let it sit for a short time. The sequence of lifting, pausing, and reeling would be repeated until a fish took the bait or the retrieve was competed.

During much of the sequence the jig is dropping or sitting, and most often this is when the bass would hit. The takes are very subtle, not the no-doubt slams felt when a crank or spinner bait is burned in. There were two ways to detect when a fish took the jig when it was dropping or sitting on the bottom. If the lighting was favorable, I would watch where the line entered the water and if a bass took the jig the line would twitch, or if the bass swam off with the jig the line would move in the direction the bass was swimming. If the line moved in an unnatural manner, I would set the hook. At the same time I would be feeling for sensations in the rod grip. When a bass took the jig, a signal would be sent up the line and into the rod and would be felt in the grip as little ticks or taps, or there might be a slight tightening of the line. Bass can be caught on a jig and trailer steadily reeled in, but it is not nearly as effective as when the bait is fished passively with lots of drops and pauses.

**Facing:** Nice rainbow from the Yampa River that couldn't resist a passively fished Virile Meat Whistle. The Yampa has been documented to have more than a dozen real virile crawdads per square meter. If you feel some nips or taps but do not hook up, try a rapid series of hand twists. Even a dying animal often has one last burst of energy if it is about to get eaten and can give a burst of speed, which can trigger a grab. These little nips at the tail of the rabbit strip most often are experienced when trout fishing. Bass, even small ones, will inhale the entire fly, and most taps without hooking up are from bluegill or other brim. LANDON MAYER PHOTO

**Top left:** A handsome largemouth caught on a Virile Meat Whistle on a magical fall day in Colorado. I like to fish for bass in the spring as the water is warming up until they finish spawning. After the spawn many of the adult bass become low-light and nocturnal feeders and it is difficult to pattern them. I will start fishing for them again in the fall as the water starts cooling and the bass again become active during the day. Instinctively they know that winter is coming and they need to consume lots of calories because there is less prey available in the winter and they become less active in the cold water.

**Bottom left:** I regularly hook species other than bass while targeting bass, and one of the reasons I like the Meat Whistle is that it works so well for multiple species, which is why it is the only streamer I use when fishing warm water. Many of the trophy bluegills I catch take a 3/0 Meat Whistle while I am bass fishing. Most ponds don't have very many or any truly large bluegills, and when I land one it is truly special. I have no idea how they get it in their mouth, but somehow they manage.

**Center:** A seasoned smallmouth that has seen it all but couldn't resist a passively fished Meat Whistle. The late light almost makes the fish glow.

**Bottom right:** A nice wiper hooked inadvertently while bass fishing.

**Top right:** Late afternoon alpenglow light illuminating the magnificent cat, a fish that has endurance, is powerful, and is a worthy adversary on a fly rod. In Colorado most ponds and many lakes have channel catfish, and hopping a Meat Whistle along the bottom using the passive streamer technique is one of the best ways to hook one. Channels cannot be targeted but I have caught a fair number of them inadvertently while bass fishing, so it is a legitimate way to hook one. Like bass, channel cats love crawdads, and a Meat Whistle is a really good crawdad imitation.

177

I had confidence that the Meat Whistle was an effective pattern and felt it could be fished in a similar manner to how I fished the jig and trailer, but I wasn't sure how to do it. A big problem I faced was how to detect when a fish took the fly when it was sinking or sitting on the bottom. Step one was figuring out what kind of line and leader setup to use. I thought about old-school nymph fishing in rivers when I would watch the end of my floating line for movement when a fish took a nymph and thought the same principle might apply when fishing stillwaters. I reasoned that if a fish took a fly that was dropping or sitting on the bottom, I may not feel the take but the floating line would serve as a strike indicator. Also the floating line would lift the fly off the bottom during the retrieve, and when the retrieve paused the fly would fall back to the bottom. I decided that a hi-vis floating line would be the best choice to accomplish these objectives.

The leader and tippet were important but not as critical as choosing the right line. I had always used 7½-foot 0X leaders and 0X tippet when bass fishing, and that is what I would use for the new setup. I wanted the line to remain floating when the fly was sinking and sitting on the bottom, so I decided the deeper the water, the longer the tippet would need to be. I liked the setup, and it was time for some field-testing.

First I would have to see if takes could be detected by watching the line for movement as the fly was dropping or sitting on the bottom. I found that when a fish took the Meat Whistle when it was sinking or sitting, the line would move in an unnatural manner. I was so used to stripping streamers on a tight line and feeling the hit that I had to train myself to constantly focus on the line, just like watching an indicator when nymph fishing. If I saw any unnatural movement of the line, I would strip-set hard. Sometimes the line would just twitch, and sometimes it would move if the fish started swimming with the fly in its mouth. The rabbit, marabou, and Sili Legs must feel natural to bass, because they will often swim off with the fly and not spit it out.

It sounds easy and straightforward, but it took a while before I developed confidence that when the line moved it was usually a fish that caused the movement, and early in the process I was surprised every time I hooked a fish. Success builds confidence, and after a while I expected to hook a fish when I saw the line move. I try to watch the tip of the line, but if the tip isn't visible, I watch the part of the line closest to the fly that I can see.

Detecting takes when I couldn't clearly see the line because of glare or otherwise poor lighting was a bigger challenge. When a fish takes a jig or a fly, little taps or ticks are generated up the line. When I use a casting or spinning reel, the line is wound in directly onto the reel and the taps are

**Facing:** A passively fished rust Slumpbuster fooled this muscular rainbow on the Yampa River in Steamboat, Colorado. When passively fishing a streamer in a river, I cast slightly upstream and let the fly sink. As the fly is carried downcurrent I stay in contact with the fly by hand twisting and/or stripping the line, while including frequent pauses throughout the drift. Pausing allows the fly with its tungsten cone to sink, while hand twisting or stripping causes the fly to rise up. This technique is most effectively fished with a hi-vis floating line. When the tip of the line moves in an unnatural manner, I make a hard strip. If a fish isn't hooked I continue the drift and let the fly swing until it is straight below me and then pick up and make another cast. LANDON MAYER PHOTO

Showing how I grip the line with my left hand while retrieving using the hand-twist technique. JAKE BURLESON PHOTO

While retrieving the fly I leave the line draped over the first crease on the middle finger of my rod hand to help detect takes when the fly is dropping or sitting on the bottom. I feel for any ticks or tightening of the line against the finger or anything that feels different. JAKE BURLESON PHOTO

transmitted into the rod grip and are easily detected by the rod hand. When a fish takes a fly that isn't being retrieved, the same taps are generated into the fly line but not the rod grip because the line is stripped in and not reeled onto the reel. How to feel these taps in the line was a challenging problem.

When fly fishing, when line is retrieved it is usually held against the grip with a finger on the rod hand and is stripped in with the other hand. When a streamer is stripped on a tight line and the line is pinched against the cork, it is easy to feel when a fish strikes. When a fish takes a fly that is dropping or sitting on the bottom, it sends very subtle signals through the line, but I had a difficult time detecting these signals when the line was pinched against the cork. I had to find a new way to handle the line so that these subtle takes could be consistently detected.

The technique I developed was a departure from how fly fishers normally retrieve line, but when fishing a streamer passively it proved to be very effective. I extend the middle finger of my rod hand away from the grip and just drape the line over the palm-side crease below the first knuckle. Instead of stripping the line, I gather line by hand twisting, much like the classic chironomid retrieve except the line is just sitting in the finger crease and not pinched against the cork. When a fish takes the fly, little ticks or taps or sometimes just a slight tightening is felt on the finger that the fly line is draped over. I learned to strip-set hard whenever the line felt different against the finger. During the retrieve I simultaneously watch the line for movement and feel for any changes in the line draped over my finger.

One of the big advantages of hand twisting the line is the line is constantly gripped by the retrieving hand and the fly can be instantly strip-set when the line moves or any changes are felt. If a fish is not hooked on the strip-set, the retrieve is just continued. If I feel a touch or a nip but do not hook the fish, sometimes I will make a few quick hand twists or a conventional strip and continue hand twisting. The sudden quick movement of the fly can trigger a fish to return to the fly, often with an aggressive take. A big advantage of fishing a fly where the hook point rides up is it is far less likely to hang up on something on the bottom and it will come through weeds better than a fly that rides with the hook point down.

In summary, I cast the fly and let it sink. While the fly is sinking I watch the line for movement and stay alert for any changes felt in the finger that the line is draped over. After letting the fly sit on the bottom for a short time, I start the retrieve with a hand twist, which lifts the fly off of the bottom, followed by a pause, which lets the fly fall back to the bottom. The floating line lifts the fly during the twist, and the weighted fly causes it to fall during the pause. I will continue this pattern where the fly is lifted and allowed to drop until a fish takes the fly or the retrieve is completed. Many of the takes from both bass and trout occur as the fly is dropping after the cast or when the retrieve is paused. I will try a variety of retrieves, often during the same cast. I will mix in several slow or rapid hand twists or maybe a traditional strip before pausing. Sometimes I will raise the rod tip and lower it, which causes the fly to rise up and fall more dramatically than with just a hand twist.

A gorgeous brown that couldn't pass up a Virile Meat Whistle passively fished during the fall on the Yampa River in Steamboat, Colorado. Have patience when learning the passive technique. It takes time to develop confidence, which will come when you start catching fish, and with practice the technique will become second nature. JAY NICHOLS PHOTO

One of my favorite retrieves is a hand twist with a sharp snap at the end of the twist, followed by a pause. The retrieve is executed with the hand and wrist, and almost no arm movement. It is like the familiar chironomid hand twist, but at the end you quickly increase the speed of the twist and finish with a quick, rotational snap of the wrist. During the twist the fly slowly rises, and the snap gives it a short darting movement followed by the drop. There is

something about the rising, darting motion followed by the falling motion during the pause that triggers takes. Towards the end of the retrieve I sweep the fly through the water with the rod tip before picking it up. This gives the fly a burst of speed, which can trigger a "don't let it get away" response from a following fish.

You never know what retrieve may trigger a take. After countless hours on the water, the technique of watching and feeling the line became second nature and I began to have unbelievable success catching sub-surface bass.

I felt confident that the new technique was effective, but the real test was to fish the Meat Whistle head to head with the jig and trailer. I spent a significant part of a season from March through October fishing both a conventional rod with a jig and trailer and a fly rod with a Meat Whistle. I carried both the conventional and fly gear with me in the float tube, and switched back and forth after a fish was caught. As the season progressed, my excitement grew as the Meat Whistle was matching the jig and trailer for both size and numbers of bass, and when the season ended the Meat Whistle fished passively with the fly gear proved to be as effective as the skirted jig and trailer fished passively with conventional gear.

I developed and learned the passive streamer technique while fishing the Meat Whistle for bass in stillwaters, but found that the Meat Whistle and the technique were equally effective for stillwater trout. Adult trout are predators and like bass are always on the lookout for injured and vulnerable prey. Trout love flies that are fished slowly with lots of drops. Crawdads live in many of our coldwater lakes and rivers and trout, especially the large ones, are always on the lookout for the highly nutritious craw, and the Meat Whistle is an almost perfect crawdad imitation. In some lakes and rivers crawdads are the primary forage for the larger trout.

When fishing for bass and trout in still-waters, I use the passive technique almost exclusively. In rivers I fish both traditional tight-line and passive techniques. I usually use the same hi-vis line, 7½-foot 0X leader, 0X tippet, and weighted Meat Whistle when fishing rivers that I do when fishing stillwaters, which gives me the option of using both the traditional and passive techniques. I still swing and retrieve the fly but also mix in the passive technique. During a drift on a tight line I will push the rod towards the fly, which puts slack in the line and leader, which lets the fly dive down.

I will let the fly dive anywhere during the drift, but I especially like to let it dive down into fishy water along the bank, behind boulders, into depressions in the river bottom, or where a riffle drops into a run. Trout can be anywhere in a run, but these areas can be especially productive. As the fly is dropping, I am watching the end of the line for movement as well as feeling for takes.

There are slow, deeper sections of rivers often referred to as "frog water" that fly fishers often pass up or don't fish seriously, but these runs can hold large trout and can be surprisingly productive using the passive approach. Slow side channels, back bays, and eddies can be effectively fished with the passive technique. Whenever possible you want the fly to sink to the bottom where trout look for crayfish, sculpins, and large nymphs.

When fishing rivers it is not always possible to incorporate the passive technique, but I like to use it whenever I can. I still use a high-density sink tip in some rivers that have a strong current and where much of the productive water is deep. The Meat Whistle can be fished on the bottom of the river with minimal hang-ups because the hook point rides up. A standard J hook

Landon Mayer spotted this northern pike in the Yampa River and had to hand-twist a Virile Meat Whistle in front of it. The pike viciously attacked the streamer, and Landon luckily hooked the fish with the 0X tippet outside the toothy mouth and was able to land it. He had the rig hooked up for trout. JAY NICHOLS PHOTO

pattern with the hook point riding down cannot be fished on the bottom without frequent snagging and damage to the hook point from rocks.

As I was developing the passive streamer technique, I used the Meat Whistle without a trailer, but now I usually fish a trailer tied on an 18- to 24-inch section of 0X or 1X fluorocarbon tippet tied off the bend of the Meat Whistle. Any streamer can be used as the trailer, but my favorite is an unweighted Slumpbuster. When wet the profile of a Slumpbuster is a good imitation of a baitfish or a juvenile crawdad, and an unweighted streamer will have a different action and swim a little higher in the water than the weighted Meat Whistle.

I like fishing the food-rich zone on or near the bottom in both still and flowing waters, but fish will suspend throughout the water column and anywhere in the column can be productive. In stillwaters, if I am not hooking fish near the bottom, instead of letting the fly sink to the bottom after making a cast, I will start the passive retrieve shortly after making the cast. I will repeat the hand-twist pause retrieve while allowing the fly to sink deeper until the retrieve is finished. This allows me to target fish throughout the water column. Try fishing different depths until you find the fish. There is no wrong way to fish the technique, so feel free to experiment.

I use the same setup when fishing for trout or bass: a fast-action 6-weight rod, a hi-vis WF floating 6-weight line with a taper that has most of the weight concentrated towards the front of the head, and a 7½-foot 0X leader with a 0X fluorocarbon tippet. If it is sunny and the water is clear, I sometimes use 1X. The relatively heavy tippet facilitates turning over the heavy fly and allows me to strip-set hard without fear of breaking off the fish. I have not noticed a problem getting takes from trout or bass using the heavy tippet, even from pressured fish. Maybe fish get a bit more excited and are less cautious when they see a substantial meal, and they don't notice the heavy tippet like they do with nymphs and dry flies.

I use a five-turn clinch knot to attach the streamer to the tippet. Some fly fishers swear by a loop knot, and in theory it gives the fly more freedom to move, which is probably true, but I am not convinced that a streamer tied on with a loop knot is more effective than one tied on with a clinch knot, and a clinch knot is a lot easier and quicker to tie and to consistently tie perfectly. Knots that are not tied properly will fail. Both clinch and loop knots work well, and I recommend using the knot you have the most confidence in.

A good reason to fish streamers where the hook point rides up is it greatly reduces the potential for disfiguring a fish's mouth. Almost every bass and trout I have hooked on a fly where the hook point rides up is hooked in the top of the mouth, which causes very little damage to the fish. A fly tied on a J hook where the point rides down will hook most fish in the corner or bottom of the mouth, including the tongue. Most disfiguring occurs when a fly, including barbless flies, buries in the cartilaginous and bony corner. The damage can occur when the fly is removed no matter how careful you are. Also the tissue on the sides and bottom of the mouth, including the tongue, is very vascular and is where most bleeding occurs when the fly is removed. The reality is when a fish is hooked anywhere there will be damage, but the impact is greatly reduced if the fish is hooked in the top of the mouth. It is somewhat irrelevant when a fish is hooked on a small nymph or dry fly, but most streamers are tied on large hooks and where the hook embeds in a fish's mouth is relevant.

The passive streamer technique takes time to learn and perfect. You have to train yourself to watch the line and feel for the subtle taps, and you need to hook some fish to develop confidence. If you stick with it, however, positive results will follow, and in time the technique will become second nature.

# WINNING COMBINATIONS: PUTTING IT ALL TOGETHER

This final chapter is a hodgepodge of different aspects of fly fishing that I have thought long and hard about, and that I don't feel have been discussed all that much. Having the right flies is simply not enough. There are a number of other things that are also important, and are much more elusive.

It's important to stay focused not just when you are casting to the fish, but through the entire fight. Maximum pressure and control is best achieved by keeping the rod in a fairly low position. The only time I have my rod tip up is so the leader can clear some structure while a fish is running or to stay tight on a fish while fighting a fish that swims towards me. JAKE BURLESON PHOTO

The mental aspect is rarely thought about or discussed, but it plays an integral role in our fly-fishing success. We have all heard that 10 percent of anglers catch 90 percent of the fish. I'm not sure where that stat came from, but the point is that a small percentage of fly fishers regularly outfish others. There are no real secrets when it comes to fly patterns, equipment, and where to fish, and I feel that one of the most important elements that separates the 10 percenters from the 90 percenters is their superior mental game.

Sports such as football, basketball, baseball, and golf require skill and expertise to perform at a high level, and I view fly fishers as athletes whose sport is fly fishing. Fly fishing is not as difficult as hitting a golf ball or a 100 mph fastball, but a basic skill set is still required. Athletes, including fly fishers, who consistently perform at a high level are often those that have the best mental skills.

## Develop Brain Two

When you have to make a precise cast to a big brown sipping PMDs 6 inches off a bank in flat water, it can be much more difficult than hitting a target on the grass while practicing golf in your backyard. If a big bonefish is coming across a flat and almost in casting range and you have one chance to make a good cast, many fly fishers blow the cast that they are fully capable of making. There is a reason good casters choke when making a cast under pressure.

Sian Beilock, a psychology professor at the University of Chicago, wrote a book titled *Choke*, which scientifically analyzes why athletes blow it. Beilock and other scientists who study choking concluded that athletes choke under stress when too many thoughts flood the prefrontal cortex, which is the part of the brain that is responsible for conscious thinking. While executing an athletic movement the only part of the brain that should be active is the motor cortex, which stores muscle memory and subconsciously controls the execution of movements. I like to think of the part of the brain that consciously thinks and analyzes, the pre-frontal cortex, as Brain One and the subconscious part that stores the muscle memory, the motor cortex, as Brain Two.

A good day on the water does not consist of just fishing. Observing various flora and fauna, enjoying the companionship of friends, and just enjoying the day are also important. However, when we are actually fishing, we need to stay laser focused. Every cast must have a purpose and not just aimlessly launched. The fly must be consistently placed where you think there are fish, and presented so the drift is good and your fly has the best opportunity to get eaten by a fish. When your dry fly or indicator is floating down the river, never take your eyes off of it. If you lose your focus and look around, invariably you will miss a take. Focusing is a conscious behavior controlled by Brain One and is not that difficult.

When athletes talk about being "in the zone" or "unconscious," they are able to shut down the conscious thoughts in Brain One and let Brain Two run the show. They sometimes have no memory of what they did. In experiments, scientists have shown that when top athletes start consciously thinking about details of their technique instead of just letting Brain Two control

It's critical to practice off the water so that you develop proper muscle memory to deliver an accurate cast when needed.
JAY NICHOLS PHOTO

their actions, they tend to mess up. There are many athletes, including fly fishers, who possess the physical tools and ability to execute flawlessly, but when they need to perform under pressure they sometimes perform poorly. A big reason is the athlete starts firing up Brain One and thinking about the mechanics of what they are about to do or have thoughts of failing.

When repetitively practicing a physical action, muscle memory is stored in the subconscious section of the brain, or Brain Two, and if left alone Brain Two has the ability to execute a physical action flawlessly with no conscious thoughts involved. An important concept to remember is when Brain One is active it can neurologically interfere with the capabilities of Brain Two to accurately send its stored information to the muscles. If you consciously think about the mechanics of what you are doing while executing an athletic move, whether it is swinging a golf club or casting a fly rod, you will probably screw it up.

The best basketball players can sink free throws in their sleep, but when the game is on the line and they need to sink a free throw for the win, if they consciously start thinking about their mechanics or "if I miss we lose and the team and fans will hate me," they often clunk the shot or even worse, shoot an air ball. The same is true in football when a kicker needs to make a kick to win a game and he allows Brain One to get active as he lines up for the winning kick. He has made the same kick countless times in practice without consciously thinking about it. When he lines up for the game-winning kick, if he starts thinking of the mechanics and how horrific it will be if he misses, there is a good chance he will blow it.

Many a short putt has been missed on the golf course by world-class golfers when the tournament is on the line. In golf the inability to make a putt or other shots when the pressure is on is often referred to as the "yips" and can get so bad that careers have ended because of it.

Athletes, including fly fishers, who are "clutch" performers and can execute at a high level under pressure have the ability to shut down the conscious thinking from Brain One and let Brain Two take over while performing. In order for Brain Two to store the muscle memory and neurologically fire

Focus is one of the most important skills a fly fisher can have. JAKE BURLESON PHOTO

the muscles controlling a particular action with no conscious thoughts involved, that action must be repeated countless times. When first learning a physical action, conscious thought is necessary and the movements can be somewhat mechanical. During countless repetitions the action is slowly imprinted into Brain Two, and at some point the imprint becomes permanent and the body can perform that action with no conscious thought process.

We can all remember when we learned to ride a bike. At first it was awkward and mechanical, but after time muscle memory became ingrained into Brain Two and we could jump on the bike and ride proficiently with no conscious thoughts. Good golfers hit thousands of balls on the practice range so that when they are on the course, they can execute a shot with no conscious thoughts going through their brain while swinging.

The most important muscle memory that fly fishers require is that which allows us to consistently make quality casts with no conscious thoughts. When a giant permit is swimming into range and you have one chance to make a quality cast, muscle memory that has been embedded through practice (this is a key phrase) will allow you to just pull the trigger and make the cast without thinking about it. Some deep breaths before making a pressure cast can help free up the neurological pathways from Brain Two to the casting muscles. A friend told me about a simple but surprisingly effective technique to free up Brain Two. He just says "F–k it" before making a pressure cast.

## 10,000 Hours of Practice

Before ingraining a casting stroke into Brain Two, it is essential that you acquire good casting mechanics. Many different fly-casting styles are effective and everyone has their own style and rhythm, but there are certain principles that all good casters adhere to. Countless pages have been written about fly-casting technique that break down every facet of casting. Good written instruction is helpful, but a good casting stroke is best achieved through instruction from someone who thoroughly understands the principles involved in making a good cast. It is essential that you have good technique before you start imprinting a casting stroke into Brain Two. If you have already imprinted bad casting technique into Brain Two, you will have to learn a new casting stroke that has good technique, practice it, and through repetition hope that the muscle memory of the new technique replaces that of the bad technique.

According to Malcolm Gladwell in his book *Outliers*, to achieve elite status in any endeavor whether it is music, athletics, or anything else, no matter how much natural ability a person has, a minimum of 10,000 hours of practice is necessary before achieving elite status. Fortunately a good casting stroke is easier to achieve than becoming a virtuoso on the violin and can be attained with fewer than 10,000 hours of practice.

The point is that to ingrain the muscle memory for a good casting stroke into Brain Two, you must practice. If you have good technique imprinted into your Brain Two, you will have the confidence to make a quality cast with no conscious thought. It is no big deal if the cast is not always perfect, but you will make far more good casts if you let Brain Two run the show without interference from conscious thoughts of Brain One. If you consciously hope you make a good cast, start thinking of casting mechanics, try to aim it and hope you don't blow it, the cast often ends poorly. Remember that all things are difficult before they are easy, and once you have the casting stroke embedded into Brain Two you can train yourself to cut off conscious thoughts before or during the cast and your percentage of excellent casts under pressure will greatly increase.

There are two fundamental breakdowns that I regularly see while on the water with other fly fishers, and they are easy to correct. One is bending the wrist too much. When the wrist flexes too much during the cast it creates wide loops in the fly line and leader, which decreases line speed and robs the cast of distance and accuracy.

The second is overpowering the cast, which is the result of putting too much muscle and effort into the stroke than is necessary. When I watch elite casters, I always say to myself how easy they make it look. Besides impeccable timing and flawless technique, a big reason their casts look effortless is they do not overpower their cast. Overpowering the cast produces poor results, including "wind knots" and tailing loops where the fly lands back along the leader instead of at the target. I tend to overpower casts without realizing it, especially with light rods, and I have to consciously make myself slow down and not use too much force. Today's rods perform so well that very little effort is needed to execute a quality cast.

## Confidence Is Key

Some people are inherently confident no matter the circumstances, but regardless of one's mental makeup the confidence of most fly fishers goes up and down depending on many variables. Some, such as weather and water conditions, are beyond our control, but there are things that we can do and things to be aware of that are real confidence builders. An obvious one that relates to the discussion above about Brain Two is casting. Become a good caster and your confidence improves.

Another confidence builder is before you start fishing, make sure your tackle is in good order. Not having to worry about any aspect of your tackle while fishing gives you peace of mind and confidence and lets you focus on fishing.

The drag on your reel needs to be set properly, and the line should be in good shape and clean. The leader must not be damaged or cut too far back. If the leader is cut too far back it won't perform as it should, and if the leader doesn't turn over cleanly it can damage your confidence in making a good presentation. If your leader is regular monofilament and you are tying your fly directly to the tip of the leader, you can just add regular monofilament tippet as needed and keep using the leader until it is damaged and needs to be replaced.

I almost always use fluorocarbon tippet, and after replacing numerous tippets and cutting the tip of the regular monofilament leader back each time, it reaches a point where the discrepancy of the diameter between the leader and the tippet can get so great that I don't feel confident in the fluorocarbon-to-monofilament blood knot and I put on a new leader. The final 2 feet of most leaders is the diameter stated on the leader package, so quite a few new tippets can be added before replacing the leader. Pieces of regular monofilament can be added to re-create the original-length leader before adding the fluorocarbon tippet, but I like to have one knot between my leader and tippet because it is cleaner and less confusing than having multiple knots.

Before you start fishing, check your leader and tippet and make sure there are no nicks or wind knots. Check every knot from your leader to the fly to make sure they are tied perfectly and well seated. The leader and tippet are the lifeline between you and the fish. The leader must be the right length to cast well, and all of the knots must be perfectly in order to fish with confidence.

Fly fishers often fail to check the hook point or the hook bend on a fly until they have failed to hook several fish when the take was solid or lost a fish that they thought was hooked well. While fishing, hook points can get dinged from rocks or hitting your fly rod while casting. If the point has been dulled or rolled over, the odds of hooking a fish are slim. It is easy to check the hook by sticking the hook point in your thumbnail. If it sticks, the point is fine, but if it slides off, it is damaged and the fly should

The leader and tippet are the lifeline between you and the fish. The leader must be the right length to cast well, and all of the knots must be perfectly in order to fish with confidence. JAY NICHOLS PHOTO

be changed or the hook sharpened. Hook bends can be opened up from a big fish or while pulling the fly out of wood. Even if the hook is opened slightly, fish will be lost or not even hooked. Hooks should be checked regularly in order to have confidence that they will perform properly.

## Keep It Simple

I love flies. I get a good dopamine surge just looking at flies in the bins at a fly shop. I like looking at rows of flies in my boxes and in other fly fishers' boxes. Besides looking cool, carrying a good selection of flies when you set out for a day on the water gives you confidence that you will be prepared for whatever the river or lake presents. Most fly fishers have confidence patterns that they have had success with, but the flies you carry are a constantly evolving process and one of the fun aspects of fly fishing. There is always a new pattern that is deadly that you need to add to your box. I like to keep it simple and not make things more complicated than they need to be. The reality is most of the time fly fishing is not that difficult, and many of the perceived complexities are more imagined than real.

I would guess that over the years many fly fishers accumulate an amazing amount of fly-fishing-related gear that just keeps piling up, with much of it sitting unused for years. Some people just can't stand to part with anything and they just keep adding to their storage bins. I am a great believer in the philosophy put forth in Marie Kondo's book *The Life Changing Magic of Tidying Up: The Japanese Art of Decluttering and Organizing*. She calls it the KonMari method.

The basic premise of her book is that if your space is kept tidy and decluttered, all aspects of your life will be far better. The secret is to start by discarding then organizing your space thoroughly and completely.

The book focuses on decluttering and organizing your house, apartment, or workplace, but the philosophy without question can be applied to your fly-fishing gear. Among the many things that accumulate are rods and reels that are never used, old fly lines and tippet, old waders, rain gear that leaks, etc. Some things need to be discarded, whereas others such as rods and reels can be sold or donated to various groups.

I highly recommend starting every season by discarding your old tippet and replacing it with new spools. You never know when something may have inadvertently gotten on your tippet, such as DEET turning your 5X into 8X, and it just gives you peace of mind knowing your tippet is new and fresh and that the spools are fully loaded.

The KonMari method can definitely be applied to the number of flies we carry while on the water. Most of us have home waters that we fish often and we know what patterns we might need. That is all you need to have with you. You don't need to bring numerous boxes holding every fly you own. The flies you need to carry vary with what species you are targeting, where you are fishing, and what time of year you are fishing, and I recommend that you change out the flies you carry accordingly. I am not saying to discard flies, but rather keep them at home in well-organized boxes. I have separate storage boxes for dry flies, nymphs, spinners, pupas, emergers, streamers, and bass patterns. If you want to remove or add

Landing fish. JAKE BURLESON PHOTO

some flies to your boxes, you have a good system to do so.

Being tidy and organized is not for everyone, but I think most fly fishers would benefit by adopting some form of the KonMari philosophy.

## Master the Methods

Using an appropriate fly pattern is very important, but how you fish it is just as important. Good technique and good fly patterns go hand in hand. The technique you use plays an important role in fishing with confidence. If you use a technique with which you have had success and that you are proficient at, you will fish that technique with confidence. Many fly fishers are proficient in a number of techniques, but they may have one or two that they are the most confident in and enjoy fishing whenever possible.

Usually a number of different techniques will be successful on a given day on a given river. For example, my favorite technique is to fish dry-dropper combos to rising fish, but most often there are no rising fish and I usually fish the Hopper-Copper-Dropper technique, which I totally enjoy and have maximum confidence in. Many anglers fish with lots of confidence when nymph fishing using an indicator, for good reason. It is often a very effective technique.

Other options include the insanely deadly Euro nymphing technique, which I have tried but not mastered; thus I have minimal confidence in the technique. Those who have serious Euro skills fish the technique with massive confidence, primarily because they catch so many fish. Most fly fishers fish streamers in high or off-colored water or when fishing for aggressive spawners, but a skilled and confident streamer fly fisher may choose to fish streamers in any conditions.

All techniques will catch fish, but the more proficient and successful you are with any of the techniques, the more confidence you will have when fishing them.

## Prep

A productive day on the water starts with good preparation. Before leaving home, double check to make sure you have *everything* you might need. We have all started a day on the water and realized we had forgotten something critical like waders or fly rods. I have one spot where I keep my waders, wading belt and boots, net, vest, and rods. I try to always keep essentials such as important fly boxes, tippet material, nippers, fly floatant, and hemostats in my vest at all times.

An important and fun part of preparation is deciding what flies to carry and what fly boxes to organize them in. There are some patterns that I carry at all times, and others that are added or removed depending on the season, the aquatic insect activity that is anticipated, and where I am going. If I am fishing familiar waters I know what patterns I will need, and my boxes will contain all of them. I will carry a few of the patterns I might need and large numbers of the ones I know that I will be using a lot.

There are some patterns that I always carry, such as Copper Johns and Barr Emergers because they are two of my max confidence patterns and can be used throughout the year. I always carry a good supply of hoppers in different sizes throughout the season because I fish the HCD technique so often. Other patterns such as PMD duns and emergers and Tricos, for example, are more seasonal and I will add them when I anticipate those insects hatching. I always carry a few streamers and will increase the supply if I think that streamers might be a good option. If I am going to fish waters I am not familiar with, I will do some research to decide what patterns I need to add. There are countless different fly patterns, and the important thing is to have patterns to cover the different scenarios you might encounter so that you can confidently fish those scenarios.

I do the majority of my freshwater fishing using three rods. I like 9-foot fast-action graphite rods in 3-, 4-, and 6-weight. I use the 3-weight when fishing hatches in rivers, and the 4-weight when nymph fishing with an indicator in lakes and rivers, fishing hatches in lakes, and fishing the HCD. I use the 6-weight when streamer fishing for trout and fishing topwater or subsurface for bass. I like a 7½-foot 3-weight fast-action graphite

You will fish, and fight fish, with much more confidence if you know your tackle's limits. You can often add much more pressure than you think when fighting a fish.
JAKE BURLESON PHOTO

I have a tippet T attached to each side of my vest to hold tippet spools. I attach a pair of nippers to both of them with 60-pound nylon. One tippet holder has 3X to 6X fluorocarbon; the second has 0X to 2X. JAKE BURLESON PHOTO

rod when fishing small streams, and a 9-foot 8-weight fast-action graphite rod when fishing for northern pike.

I usually carry the 3-, 4-, and 6-weight rods in double rod cases with me all of time, with a second 4-weight rod in case I break one of the rods while fishing. If necessary I can dry-fly or streamer fish with the 4-weight. I carry backup reels with 3-, 4-, and 6-weight lines in case I damage a reel I am using. I am a big believer in carrying backups of the essentials with me while on the water.

I carry a ziplock bag in the back of my vest with 3X to 6X tippet, 7½-foot 0X and 2X and 9-foot 5X leaders, nippers, fly floatant, hemostats, and sunglasses—and lots of water (hydration is very important). I also have a Tie-Fast tool in the ziplock in case I lose a leader, which has happened to me twice when an unstoppable fish took off through a bunch of logs and branches. I was really happy to have an extra leader and the Tie-Fast tool with me. I know hemostats can be used, but the tool is easier and small and light.

Being organized and well prepared gives you peace of mind and allows you to totally enjoy the day and just focus on fishing.

## Timing

All fisheries, both lakes and rivers, have their prime times which often coincide with aquatic insect hatches, and hitting a fishery during these times generates instant confidence. You know what fly patterns you will need, and knowing that the fish will be actively feeding is a huge confidence builder. Anticipating and hitting a hatch perfectly is one of the great pleasures for a fly fisher. Many trips are planned around a particular hatch or a time of year when multiple species are hatching.

Another prime-time confidence builder is when fish in a lake are getting ready to spawn and after they enter the river to spawn. Traditionally rainbows and cutthroats spawn in the spring and browns in the fall. The fish can be very active and aggressive as they stage at the mouth of the river where they are going to spawn, and fishing this zone can be very productive and

Fish can be caught any time of the year, but fishing during prime times for each species is the most productive and will definitely elevate the level of confidence. JAKE BURLESON PHOTO

Right after ice-out on a reservoir, big trout will often cruise near the shoreline looking for forage. I spotted this tuna-strong chromer cruising the edge in Antero Reservoir near Fairplay, Colorado, in the spring shortly after ice-out. This is an example where timing adds to confidence. LANDON MAYER PHOTO

fished with confidence. Once they enter the river these spawners can be prime targets for the fly fisher, and can often be larger than the resident fish in the river. Having a river full of large and aggressive fish is a real confidence builder.

A variable that affects confidence is fishing familiar water versus unfamiliar water. Although every day is a little different, even on familiar water, you know what techniques to use, what flies to carry, where the productive runs are, when to expect certain hatches, and where to look for rising fish. On unfamiliar water you can certainly be successful if you can read water and have the right skills, but all lakes and rivers have their own little idiosyncrasies and knowing where to fish the most productive water, especially in a lake, can be challenging. Hiring a guide is a really good idea if you want to fish a new river or lake with confidence and maximize your day.

Other variables beyond your control such as water and weather conditions can affect confidence. Fish can be caught in high or dirty water, but the confidence is greater when fishing clear water at normal flows. I have confidence fishing during cloudy or sunny days, but probably a little more on cloudy days. Hatches can be better on cloudy days, and the fish are not as spooky as they can be when it is sunny. Confidence is higher when it is calm, but fishing can still be good if you know how to adapt to wind.

When you fish with confidence, your day will be more productive and enjoyable. Every time you make a cast your mindset should be that a fish is going to take your fly. You must get in a run, feel you are positioned perfectly, and have confidence in your fly pattern and that your leader and tippets and knots are in perfect shape and that your overall setup is poised for success. There is no doubt in your mind you can make a good presentation, and you just "know" you are going to hook a fish. If you are just hoping you might hook a fish or even worse figure there is no way you are going to hook a fish, every aspect of your fishing from your casting to your drift is going to reflect this mindset and your success will be diminished. It requires good preparation, time, and positive results to develop confidence, but when you go fishing if you carry a positive, confident attitude, good results are sure to follow.